HAUNTED
WORLD WAR II

About the Author

Matthew L. Swayne (State College, PA) is a journalist who currently works as a research writer at Penn State. He was a regular contributor to a revitalized version of *Omni* magazine, called Omni Reboot. He wrote the Anti-Matter column, which looked at fringe science and the paranormal. He has also discussed ghostlore and the unknown on numerous radio shows and podcasts, including Coast to Coast AM and Darkness Radio. Balancing skepticism with an open mind, Matt uses his experience in journalism and interest in both ghostlore and the paranormal to collect and tell stories about the supernatural.

To Write the Author

If you wish to contact the author or would like more information about this book, please write to the author in care of Llewellyn Worldwide, and we will forward your request. Llewellyn Worldwide cannot guarantee that every letter written to the author can be answered, but all will be forwarded. Please write to:

Matthew L. Swayne
⅀ Llewellyn Worldwide
2143 Wooddale Drive
Woodbury, MN 55125-2989

Please enclose a self-addressed stamped envelope for reply, or $1.00 to cover costs. If outside the USA, enclose an international postal reply coupon.

MATTHEW L. SWAYNE

HAUNTED
WORLD WAR II

Soldier Spirits, Ghost Planes &
Strange Synchronicities

Llewellyn Worldwide
Woodbury, Minnesota

FIRST EDITION
Second Printing, 2019

Book design by Bob Gaul
Cover Illustration by Dominick Finelle / The July Group
Cover design by Kevin R. Brown
Editing by Annie Burdick
All photos are from the Library of Congress Digital Collection except for P-40 on page 59 from the New York Public Library, Manuscripts and Archives Division, and Churchill on page 155 from the New York Public Library, Slavic and East European Collections

Llewellyn Publications is a registered trademark of Llewellyn Worldwide Ltd.

Library of Congress Cataloging-in-Publication Data
Names: Swayne, Matthew L., author.
Title: Haunted World War II : soldier spirits, ghost planes & strange
    synchronicities / by Matthew L. Swayne.
Description: First edition. | Woodbury, MN : Llewellyn Publications, [2018] |
    Includes bibliographical references.
Identifiers: LCCN 2018027546 (print) | LCCN 2018035817 (ebook) | ISBN
    9780738756141 (ebook) | ISBN 9780738755793 (alk. paper)
Subjects: LCSH: Ghosts. | Haunted places. | World War, 1939–1945—Miscellanea.
Classification: LCC BF1471 (ebook) | LCC BF1471 .S93 2018 (print) | DDC
    133.1/4—dc23
LC record available at https://lccn.loc.gov/2018027546

Llewellyn Worldwide Ltd. does not participate in, endorse, or have any authority or responsibility concerning private business transactions between our authors and the public.
    All mail addressed to the author is forwarded, but the publisher cannot, unless specifically instructed by the author, give out an address or phone number.
    Any Internet references contained in this work are current at publication time, but the publisher cannot guarantee that a specific location will continue to be maintained. Please refer to the publisher's website for links to authors' websites and other sources.

Llewellyn Publications
A Division of Llewellyn Worldwide Ltd.
2143 Wooddale Drive
Woodbury, MN 55125-2989
www.llewellyn.com

Printed in the United States of America

CONTENTS

Introduction   *1*

1: Haunted Battlefields, Barracks, and Bases   5

The Ghosts of Normandy's Coast   7

Ghostly Echoes on the Beaches of Dieppe   15

Other Haunted Battlefields in Western Europe   18

Not So Quiet on the Eastern Front   22

Pacific Theater: The Supernatural Sands
   of Iwo Jima   28

Okinawa's Restless Spirits   33

Eternal Return: The Spirits of the Philippines   40

2: Ghost Planes and Haunted Airfields 47

The Ghost Planes of Dark Peak   48

America's Ghost Plane Incidents   55

The Phantom Flying Fortress   60

Haunted Bases and Airfields   65

Haunts in Hawaii—Hickam Air Force Base   65

Spectral Displays at the National Museum of the United States Air Force   72

The Haunted Bomber of Cosford Aerospace Museum   80

3: Supernatural on the High Seas 89

The USS *Yorktown:* A Tourist Attraction Gets Attention from Paranormal Investigators   91

The USS *Hornet:* Raising the Dead   100

The USS *Lexington:* True Ghost Encounters Aboard the Blue Ghost   108

The USS *North Carolina:* Showboat Ghosts   117

The USS *Arizona:* Solemn Spirits of the USS *Arizona* Memorial   128

The USS *The Sullivans* (DD-537): A Haunting Family Legacy   134

4: World War II's Ghostly Leaders 143

Old Blood and Ghosts: General George S. Patton 144

Five-Star Ghost: Dwight D. Eisenhower 148

Prime Minister of the Paranormal: Winston Churchill 155

A German General's Ghost in America: Erwin Rommel 159

5: Magic Battles, Mystic Warriors, and Psychic Warfare 165

Crowley and Hitler: Battle of the Beasts 166

Witches United: How England's Witches and Wiccans United to Stop Hitler 173

US Marshals Its Spiritual Forces 180

Axis Forces: Nazi Occult Power 186

6: Fortean Forces in World War II 193

UFOs During World War II 194

Foo Fighters 195

The Battle of Los Angeles 207

The Philadelphia Experiment 212

World War II Coincidences and Curses 217

The Curse of Tamerlane 217

Precognitive Codes—Did Messages Predict
World War II Actions?   220

The D-Day Synchronicities   221

Pearl Harbor Prediction: Coded Message or
Creepy Coincidence?   225

Conclusion: Haunts, Heroes, and Hallowed Reminders   229

Notes and Bibliography   235

Chapter 1   235
Chapter 2   238
Chapter 3   242
Chapter 4   245
Chapter 5   246
Chapter 6   248

To my father, Joseph Swayne, who taught me to respect history, science, and religion, but also to never stop questioning.

INTRODUCTION

The best academic guess is that the global conflict we call World War II caused the untimely end of about sixty million men and women—civilians and soldiers. Some experts say that this is a conservative figure and place their estimates millions higher.

Whatever the exact figure—which we will never know for sure—it is hard to conceive the loss of tens of millions of lives. It's even more sobering to conceive of all the potential represented in those millions of lives that humanity lost on the shores of the Normandy coast, in the death camps of Poland, in the islands of the South Pacific, in the oceans of the North Atlantic, and in the icy trenches of the Eastern Front. Artists and musicians, laborers and craftsmen, engineers and architects, fathers and mothers, sons and daughters, all lost before they truly registered their contributions on earth.

History haunts us.

In this book, we will find out that history does more than encode their lives in rows and columns of statistics and casualty figures; it preserves them in stories—and some of those stories are ghost stories and tales of the supernatural. There are stories of battlefields in Europe and of invasion sites in the South Pacific that still seem unable, or unwilling, to let the past go; places where the spirits of soldiers, sailors, and civilians return again and again to recreate their last moments on hallowed and haunted soil. We will even discover tales not of haunted houses, but haunted ships. It seems warships preserved to be living museums have retained some of their original crews.

Ghosts on ships are one thing, but how about airplanes that become ghosts? In the skies of England, especially, the warbirds of World War II are still making glorious passes and strafing runs and have been since the end of the war, according to witnesses.

World War II has done more than just spawn some great ghost stories. With more trained observers watching the skies than at any time in history, the modern UFO era can trace its roots back to World War II. In this book, we have devoted an entire section to some of the stories of strange aircraft—or foo fighters—that crews of fighters and bombers witnessed in the skies.

We will also probe one more mystery of the war—signs and synchronicities. There's a theory that in times of danger our heightened sense of awareness can access highly refined powers of intuition and understanding. Scientists say this is just a more efficient use of natural powers of observation. Others say these are examples of psychic powers. World War II has numerous examples of these "Fortean" powers. I'll let you decide how natural—or supernatural—these powers are.

So, let's start our journey into haunted World War II with a visit to the haunted battlefields of Europe and Asia.

1

HAUNTED BATTLEFIELDS, BARRACKS, AND BASES

Even though the dark days of World War I—the war to end all wars—were just a shadow in the past, the world was unprepared for the carnage, ferocity, and genocidal terror of World War II. The fields of Europe were just recovering from the last war's wounds only to be torn anew and, in many cases, the new wounds ripped even wider and deeper. The Second World War struck targets unscathed in World War I. Asia exploded and isolated. Idyllic islands in the Pacific were not spared, either.

D-Day. Iwo Jima. Stalingrad. The Battle of the Bulge. They are names of battles that have been burned into the pages of history and into the global consciousness.

Investigators into paranormal phenomena and witnesses who have stumbled onto unexplainable events say that it's more than just the names of these battles that survive and continue to resonate decades later. These people say that the spirits of those who fought—and died—during those battles remain as well. Witnesses have heard their voices, sensed their presences, and even seen their apparitions.

In this section, we will visit some of those famous battlefields and review the spookiest supernatural encounters at those hallowed sites. We will travel with tourists who unexpectedly ran into ghosts of World War II past at memorial sites that celebrate those famous engagements and those courageous warriors. We will creep down dark paths and wander through the halls of forts and barracks with real ghost investigators who traveled to those sites to find spirit activity, but tell us that the level of activity they encountered—or maybe endured—during their explorations surprised even them.

As we journey into haunted battlefields, bases, and barracks of the war, we will try to visit as many theaters of the war as possible. Ghosts haunt sites in Europe—on both Eastern and Western Fronts—and they are rumored to haunt areas consumed by the war's unprecedented violence in the Pacific theater as well.

The first stop of our supernatural adventure is the shores of northern France, which would become the main target of the Allies' efforts to restore democracy—and which fell behind the Nazis' seemingly impregnable Atlantic Wall.

What happens when an unstoppable invasion force hits an impregnable wall?

Simple. Ghost stories happen.

The Ghosts of Normandy's Coast

If there is any World War II battlefield that deserves to be haunted, it's the sand and stone beaches of Normandy, the isolated stretch of northern France that hundreds of thousands of Allied troops stormed on June 6,1944—and which tens of thousands of those troops never left.

Since the invasion, reports of paranormal phenomena have rolled off these beaches, as regularly as the waves that once propelled the landing crafts onto the shores decades ago.

In our first story, one father writes that he is certain that his young daughter had a paranormal experience during a trip to Normandy and may have witnessed the spirit echoes of the men who fought and died there.

He writes in an online forum for military historians and military history buffs that, as someone who studied military history, he did not plan the trip to Europe as part of any ghostbusting adventure of his. It was simply a chance to see some of World War I's and World War II's most pivotal battlefields. Chief among the sites of interest were the beaches of Normandy, he said.

*A bird's-eye view of the Allied forces
landing on a Normandy beach on D-Day.*

The man, who was traveling with his wife and daughter, decided to take his seven-year-old daughter exploring in the bunkers and pillboxes that remain on Omaha Beach, arguably the bloodiest sector of the invasion. The father-daughter historical reconnaissance mission started at the bunkers of Pointe Du Hoc. In one of the many shows of Allied heroism during the D-Day invasion, a group of American rangers stormed the cliffside complex that served as an anchor for the German defenses. The fortress served as the epitome of German General Erwin Rommel's defensive genius in constructing the Nazis' Atlantic Wall to defend against just the type of incursion that the Allied generals had planned.

According to the girl's father, the excursion started out fairly typical and his daughter didn't seem to experience anything weird during their initial exploration of bunkers and "old, blown-up stuff." At least, she didn't tell her dad that she experienced any weird stuff while she toured the beach. However, later she began to tell her dad that while touring the bunker she thought she saw men. She said some of the men were armed and pointed their weapons in her direction. Other men lay on the bunker floor or crouched in the corners and crevices of the bunkers.

The father recognized that this story might just be the overactive imagination of a seven-year-old brain and didn't press her on these visions. However, about a year later, he decided to interview the girl. He assured members of the forum that prior to the visit and the year after the visit, his daughter had no—nil—exposure to his military history fascination. He didn't discuss military history. He didn't show her pictures or movies from World War II.

He added: "But one thing I will point out now...my daughter has NEVER seen what a German soldier looks like, or the weapons they carried. I have no pictures of them, nowhere in my house is there anything that she could relate to the look of them, and when I play any WWII PC games, she is not allowed to watch me, or be in the room with me (wife's orders). You get the point here? NIL EXPOSURE!!"

He began to ask his daughter about her experience at the beach. He asked what the men looked like and she began to describe the soldiers and their uniforms, which she recalled as being gray or dark green. She added that the men wore helmets that were darker than the uniforms. Her description fit historical accounts of the soldiers who would have fought at the site decades before, according to the father. She also mentioned badges and emblems on the uniforms, which matched descriptions of the ones that appeared on the uniforms of World War II soldiers.

Dad still wasn't convinced, however. He asked her for more proof.

"I asked her to draw some stuff and try to see what she saw in her head," he wrote. "What she drew scared the hell out of me."

The father explained that his daughter drew a near perfect rendition of an MP 40 (also called a Schmeisser), a German submachine gun—or machine pistol—used by some German troops in World War II. She proceeded to reliably reproduce German helmets and the tunics that German soldiers wore at about the time of the D-Day invasion.

They took a trip to the library for a follow-up. There, the father pulled out a book on World War II uniforms and weaponry. Without prompting, the little girl began to point out the items that she witnessed on the haunted beach. In a cluster of weapons used during World War II, for instance, she specifically pointed out the MP 40 gun that she described earlier.

That finally convinced dad.

"I have nothing else to think but everything she says and saw is 100 percent true," he concluded.

Other Encounters

The young girl's run-in with the spirits of Normandy isn't the only case of the supernatural remains left on the beaches of Normandy that people talk about in paranormal circles. Another witness—who goes simply by Krystal—said that she, too, had a face-to-face encounter with one of the battlefield's ghosts. Her tale may confirm the young girl's impression of a brutal battle that left more reminders than just craters and ruins of cliffside fortifications. It also left reminders through the restless dead that continue to march through the sands and over the rock formations of Normandy's beaches.

Krystal's story began on a trip to France with a group of friends. Like the father and daughter in our previous story, the love of history and the respect for the warriors who fought and died there drew them to Pointe du Hoc. From the beach, the friends noted that they could still see the remains of German bunkers and holes where bombs from Allied boats and planes had pummeled the emplacements.

Krystal and one other friend decided that a view from the beach did not satisfy their curiosity enough. Some force pulled them off the beach and perhaps into the past, into the remains of the chaotic first day of the D-Day invasion.

They just had no idea what—or who—the source of that force was. But they would soon find out.

According to the account on a message board, the last bunker they entered that morning had a strange vibration. There were no interior lights, like some of the other fortifications that allow tourists and history buffs to explore the sites in depth. There was just a little bit of light trickling in as the curious duo entered the bunker. The rest of the bunker was so dark that Krystal advised her friend to leave the bunker, find some straw and twigs, and fashion a torch.

While she waited, she heard noises coming from deep within the cavernous fortress. Like any good ranger climbing Pointe du Hoc, she did what she had to do. She charged into the bunker.

As her eyes adjusted to the darkness, she saw something coming toward her. A shadow was sweeping across the floor of the bunker and approaching her. As it got closer, Krystal made out what she presumed to be a human form. The vision stunned her. She felt paralyzed but managed to call out for her friend.

The shadow, which she could now clearly make out as a human with a hat, started to approach her, but then stopped. She watched as the figure stood near the center of the chamber before it finally began to move back into the dark section of the room, where it disappeared for good.

"After that I now believe that the ghosts of dead soldiers are still there," she writes.

Photographic Anomalies

Other visitors bring back more than stories. They bring back evidence—such as photographs and snippets of electronic voice phenomena (EVPs)—from their tours of the famous battlefield.

One man and his brother visited cemeteries and other historic spots before he visited Pointe du Hoc. He and his other friends made the same camera-happy tours of the bunkers that our other experiencers visited. In this case, however, the witnesses didn't see or detect anything out of the ordinary, at least while they were physically at the site.

It's when they left France the next day that the siblings received a supernatural shock. The man decided to flip through the photos that he snapped during their trip to Normandy. As he scanned through, he found an image he took of his brother that gave both of them shivers. The photograph seemed to show a white, somewhat transparent, but solid figure coming out of the wall of the bunker in front of the man's brother. Skeptics would possibly point to this as a camera malfunction, but the rest of the photos did not have any anomalies. The photographer adds that the image was definitely not in the viewfinder when he snapped the picture.

A newly wedded husband said he and his wife were honeymooning on Omaha Beach. Before you call that the most pathetically unromantic honeymoon ever, the husband pointed out that the wife also got her trip to Paris. But first, he decided to explore the rapidly decaying bunkers on Omaha Beach. Taking out his phone camera, the man began to snap pictures of the bunkers and the fortification's interior. Like the other "Weird War II" explorers in this section, he said that some force kept pulling him deeper into the bunker. Without electric lights, or even cracks in the wall to let the sunlight in, the room remained pitch black. He took a few steps and turned to the left, feeling his way down the long, empty corridor. At least he thought it was empty.

Eventually, the man decided to take a couple quick pictures with his flash. It satisfied two needs: it would shine some immediate light in the bunker, and he could check out the photos later. As the flashes popped off like tiny versions of the ordinance that exploded over Omaha Beach during the invasion, the man writes that he didn't notice anything out of the ordinary. During those short bursts of light, he didn't see anybody in the corridor with him. He and his wife made their way back to their hotel room in Paris.

As they settled in for the evening, they began to review photographs from their Omaha Beach visit. They immediately noticed something strange about the photos from the bunker. In one of the window-type areas, they could clearly see the haunting image of a face. Both the husband and the wife described the look on the ghost's face as "chilling."

Will these photos cause you shivers or chills? Make you a believer in the ghosts of Weird War II, or not? There are recent links in the notes and bibliography section of this book, so you can view the photographs for yourself as long as they remain posted on the web.

Ghostly Echoes on the Beaches of Dieppe

On a clear August morning in 1942, a group of commandos stormed onto the French beach near Dieppe and right into the blistering, deadly accurate gun and artillery fire from well-trained, experienced German soldiers and Kriegsmarines who had been tipped off about the raid.

Losing the element of surprise, the attack turned into a bloodbath that took the lives of about 2,500 Allied forces and resulted in thousands more being captured or wounded.

In the list of battles and raids during World War II, the Dieppe raid—officially named Operation Jubilee—typically rates as a mere footnote in the history books, an ill-fated test that failed to do anything except add a few "lessons learned" for the Allied commanders planning for D-Day. It is now just an echo lost in the thunder of bigger and more successful amphibious operations during the war, such as the Normandy invasion.

A vintage print, circa 1890–1900, of the beach at Dieppe, France.

But, whatever the history books tell or don't tell you, the heroic actions of those commandos on that August morning were apparently so powerful that you can still bear witness to the echoes of the Dieppe raid on that French beach, according to several people who claim they had supernatural experiences at the site of the former battle.

Nearly a decade after the battle, a group of families—two English women, their children, and a nurse—were vacationing near the site of the raid. In fact, the families stayed in a house that German officers once occupied. The view from the home offered a perfect vista to the beach where some of the fiercest fighting occurred. For several days, the stay remained uneventful. Then, on the morning of August 4, just a couple weeks before the anniversary of the battle, their vacation house violently shook from its placid slumber and, at least according to some occult experts, the house quite possibly shook from the very foundation of reality.

The ladies later reminisced about that morning. They said they woke up to unmistakable sounds of a violent clash. Sounds of machine gun fire and the booms of cannons echoed in the early dawn skies. The women could hear people screaming and yelling out commands. They tore out of their beds and ran to the balcony, expecting to see all hell breaking loose. Though it was still dark, they didn't see anything—no men barking orders, no guns, nothing. Stranger still, the other members of the family did not stir. They remained in bed.

As the shouts and noises faded, the women decided they could go back to bed, but struggled to process what just happened to them.

The battle sounds rose again—and then faded. In fact, over the next hour or so, the strange sounds undulated. It reached a peak shortly before dawn. And it wasn't just the sea and shore that seemed alive. The skies filled with phantoms, as well. The family claimed to hear dive bombers strafing the beach and other aircraft rumbling overhead.

During the morning's events, the ladies—though terrified—started to take notes and mark down the timing of the sounds. Later, they created reports for the British Society for Psychical Research, who investigated their claims, Strangely, the diary of events matched the Dieppe operation almost perfectly. Even the aircraft noise corresponded to the late arrival of British warplanes during the battle. The booming artillery, likewise, matched the time that destroyers began to pepper the beaches with artillery fire. Unless the women had expert knowledge of the battle, or they had a detailed history of the raid—and this was pre-internet access times, remember—there is little chance they could just guess the precise timeline of the battle. In fact, the official account of the Dieppe raid, which had been censored, and would contain the timing of the battle, was not published until a few months after the women's experience.

Most occult experts, including several members of the Society, believe that the women had a genuine supernatural encounter on this famous—and now infamously haunted—World War II battlefield.

Other Haunted Battlefields in Western Europe

Even today, decades after war raged along the Western Front of World War II, the evidence of the destruction that rained down on the land is still visible. Pockmarked fields, shattered walls, and piles of rubble are just some of the physical remains of the war. But for Tom Pedall, a ghosthunter who helps lead a paranormal investigation team from Wuppertal, Northrhine-Westfalia—which they abbreviate Ghosthunter-NRWUP—it's the spiritual remains that fascinate him and his group.

"Ghosthunting is not only a hobby for me, it is like a life task," he said, adding that he started his research in earnest back in 2001.

Pedall's interest in the field did not come from an encounter on a battlefield, at least not right way, but from an experience he had in an aunt's house in Echternach, Luxembourg, when he was about twelve.

"We heard footsteps and doors opened and closed," Pedall said. "Some years later, my parents told me that when workers were digging in the cellar, they found a skeleton—maybe that was the reason for the haunting."

He and Cloody Winterkamp, who is both his life partner and afterlife investigation partner, had several encounters with the supernatural together, which prompted their desire to find evidence of ghosts in Europe, including the spirit activities of the region's World War II battlefields. Once, for example, while living in a flat the couple heard strange noises coming from the storage area. They immediately walked toward the area to check.

No one was there.

A few nights later, though, Cloody did see something. She watched a ball of fog—about thirty to forty centimeters in diameter—appear in front of her. After that, a whole list of paranormal activity began to occur. They saw human-shaped shadows, heard noises, and noticed doors that opened and closed on their own. It wasn't just the humans in the apartment who witnessed the activity. Animals are often sensitive to supernatural forces and the couple's cats began to act and react weirdly, Tom added.

Once they saw the American television show *Ghost Hunters*, they became hooked. They realized they could both investigate the paranormal and help people. Some of the places that needed the most help included the scenes of death, trauma, and violence on the many nearby battlefields. The vast swath of land that erupted during the Battle of the Bulge in 1944 became the focus of a few of their investigations—the team became convinced that ghosts still walked portions of the hallowed ground.

Historians say that the Battle of the Bulge was a desperate last counter-offensive by Hitler's army. With the Russians blasting through the Eastern Front and the American and English forces squeezing in on the Western Front, Hitler gambled when he threw everything left in the German war machine at the Americans, taking strategic advantage of a bulge that had developed in a quiet sector of the front. They hoped to take the Americans by surprise, make a quick thrust toward the sea, and scatter the Allied supply lines. It nearly worked, but the American forces were far more tenacious than the Germans had assumed and General George Patton proved to be far quicker in an effort to relieve the troops at the Bulge. Miraculously, the weather turned favorably for the Allies, allowing the once-grounded fighters and bombers to fly missions against the German forces in the area.

Tom and Cloody's group has investigated several sections of the Bulge battlefield at least four times—with plans for more research tours soon. The site is *that* active, the group says. They guessed that Hasselpath might be one of the haunted places because much of the action swirled around the area. When the battle began, the German troops made Hasselpath one of their primary objectives—the area turned into a bloodbath. After a fierce fight, the onslaught of German armor and infantry forced the Americans to retreat and take new defensive positions on the next ridge.

The Germans used the Hasselpath corridor as a staging area for further attacks of the American lines, but did not succeed. As those attacks grew more desperate, more fierce, and more violent, the dead and wounded piled up. Tom said the team has collected evidence that some of those spirits are still on the battlefield.

During one investigation, the team used an infrared camera to take pictures of a fortification on the battlefield. When they analyzed the results, one of the images seemed to show the outline—or shadow—of a human being. Another photo seems to show a GI hunkered down in a foxhole. The team also carried a recorder in hopes of picking up electronic voice phenomena. In one snippet, the English word "peacemaker" seems to rise above the static and natural sounds of the environment.

Tom said that he may have actually seen an apparition during the investigation. He said he was startled when a person crossed the dense undergrowth just a few meters in front of him. They tried to debunk the sighting. Perhaps it was just a tourist? However, they walked to the spot of the sighting and could not locate any trace that a person moved through the area. Tom noted that the ground remained wet, but they saw no footprints.

The group plans to do more investigations of battlefields, especially at the area near the Bulge, and possibly to head to Normandy for some research there. One type of haunting is not on the team's list, though. Numerous reports that concentration camps continue to be extremely active with paranormal phenomena have circulated among the paranormal community in Europe, but Tom says the team would avoid investigations there out of respect.

"I think they are haunted, but I have too much respect for those locations," said Tom. "Respect—not like fear of the ghosts there—but I have respect for those areas because they are memorials. Very bad things happened there and it's not the correct place to make a paranormal investigation."

Not So Quiet on the Eastern Front

War exposes the darkest corners of the human soul. It is a darkness that, on one hand, disgusts us and yet also attracts—or even ensnares—our attention, on the other. Military historians say that a group of artifact collectors who seem not to be repelled by war, but enthralled by it—or at least by the war's highly profitable trophies—remain one obstacle to their ability to uncover the actual facts of World War II battlefields. They call these collectors "black archaeologists."

These battlefield scavengers scour fields and forests for guns, munitions, daggers, knives, medals, and other artifacts left over from the war. Bones, skulls, and other macabre souvenirs plucked from graves and mass graves are not necessarily outside the scope of what they will collect, either, as long as they can find a buyer.

In a few cases, however, black archaeologists on clandestine digs for war booty have encountered forces so dark and so powerful that they have accomplished the unlikely: these forces just may have scared a sense of humanity back into these hard-hearted memorabilia buzzards. One incident, according to one account, occurred in Russia, on the Eastern Front, the scene of the war's most brutal fighting.

The stories compiled in the Russian newspaper *Pravda* indicate that a group of six black archaeologists began an excavation of a site near the Makaryevsky monastery, which has more recently been turned into a convent. The monastery is near the town of Lyskovo on the banks of the Volga River.

You can only imagine the misery and atrocities that occurred during the fierce battles between German and

Soviet forces. But memories and misery could not stop this band of profiteers from camping in this hallowed site, hoping to uncover potentially profitable booty.

Initially, the hunt was unremarkable. They spent much of the day working and moving their operations closer and closer to the grounds of the monastery. However, night began to close in on them and the darkness would make further digs nearly impossible. That's when one of the team noticed a fire lighting the sky. It looked like a bonfire burning in the distance. The team decided to investigate. As they got closer, they realized that it was not a bonfire at all. It was a weird fire burning in midair. As they drew nearer, the fire faded and then stopped completely, like someone quickly snuffed it out.

The fire in the sky may have died out, but the supernatural fireworks were just starting.

Later that night, as the team bedded down for sleep, ghastly screams—definitely human—erupted in the forest. The screams unsettled the whole team. Later the next morning, one of their party entered the forest and, even though the camp was only a few feet away, became completely disoriented. He finally returned, but his friends knew quickly that something was not right. An insane expression was etched on the man's face, his eyes flashed wildly. No matter how much his friends interrogated him, he refused to tell them what he saw on his journey into the forest.

Whatever spiritual battle the souvenir-hunter fought in that forest would—like many of the other artifacts of war—remain hidden in this paranormal battlefield.

The group claimed to be happy just to make it out in one piece that morning.

A Ghost Tank Rumbles Across Russia

Another haunted spot that rests in the once battle-ridden Eastern Front is located about twenty miles from Novgorod. In 1942, thousands of Soviet soldiers attacked a formidable defensive position staffed by some of the Nazis' best-trained soldiers. In a vain attempt to relieve the Nazi stranglehold on Leningrad, the Soviets attacked the positions with little armor support, relying instead on artillery and the courage of its infantry to beat back the German soldiers and their allies. Courage and artillery were not enough, however. The offensive collapsed and the troops who were part of the maneuver to flank the Nazis became cut off and destroyed.

War relic hunters say the anguish of the battle can still be felt—and heard—in that forest. One hunter who searched the territory said that screams echoed during the night. She said it's not a solo scream of one or two practical jokers fooling around. It's as though the battle is raging all over again.

She said she could hear soldiers call out, "Hooray," as if they were on the attack. Those shouts of encouragement turned to screams of terror as the battle turned against them.

In another weird incident, the relic hunter said some force unexpectedly led her to a deadly find. While walking behind her team, something made her pause. The relic hunters had searched near that spot before, so she didn't expect to find anything new there. However, she looked into the sky and saw the trees leaning in a strange direction. The rest of the forest was still, with no discernable breeze, she said. She called out to the other members who joined her search. In no time, they uncovered a decomposed wooden box. Inside she found a stack of old land mines.

Another battlefield explorer named Alexei said that during a dig near Bryansk, they excavated the bodies of several soldiers—six Russians and eleven Germans—from a trench. Later that night, the men camped out, just a few yards from where the skeletons that they unearthed still rested. The relic hunters knew that the forest, which the locals considered sacred ground, was spooky enough at night. But now that they knew their camping site stood just a few feet from corpses of men mowed down in their prime, it took on a whole new macabre vibe.

Already on edge, the team made sure one member of the group would stand guard as the others slept. But any guard would be ineffectual against the forces the group would soon encounter. Later that night, the guard ran to the slumbering relic hunters and roused them. He heard something strange and he wanted them to verify the phenomena. Groggy but awake, they listened intently and began to make out the noises he was talking about. At first, they tried to determine the source of the sounds, but they realized these weren't just any noises; they were human voices. In hushed silence, the group soon discerned that the voices were speaking and even singing. Commands, in German, were barked out too, echoing in the forest.

It got weirder. The group may have even collected the first bit of evidence of ghost tanks. They claimed to hear the metallic clanking of treads—like those of armored vehicles—scraping along the forest floor.

The next morning, the team returned to the trenches where they uncovered the bodies. They were horrified. Next to the ditches that the team excavated the day before, they noticed fresh trenches, ones that they knew they had not dug. And, as a group of military experts, they recognized that they matched the exact specifications of anti-tank trenches.

Just when the group of war relic hunters thought it couldn't get any weirder, it got much, much weirder.

Near the trenches, they noticed fresh tracks—tank tracks.

Haunted History

In some cases, haunted history can reveal actual history. While excavating a site in the eastern section of Voronezh, researcher Genrikh Silanov told *Pravda* that he took some routine photos. When he examined the photos more closely, however, he found out that they weren't routine pictures at all. He could see ghostly figures in the shots of soldiers that definitely weren't there when he snapped them.

The photos were so clear that he could make out uniforms. As an expert on the era, he immediately recognized that one of the ghost soldiers wore a Czechoslovakian uniform. But he also knew this couldn't be—the Czechs weren't involved in this fight.

Silanov decided to investigate the matter a little more. When he did, the researcher found that, in fact, Czech units did serve—and die—in that battle. The Czechs had been integrated into Soviet units that fought there.

He also came up with a pet theory on how the ghostly images of those Czech fighters ended up in his photographs. Silanov said he believed that there is a memory field all around us and deeply emotional or violent events have the tendency to imprint on this memory field, creating *chronal mirages*, as he calls them.

Other paranormal theorists have another simpler reason: they are ghosts. Weird War II ghosts.

Pacific Theater:
The Supernatural Sands of Iwo Jima

As the war raged across the globe, once out-of-reach and remote islands became caught up in the tsunami of violence and conflict. One of those formerly peaceful spots was Iwo Jima. In Japanese, Iwo means sulfur, a smelly substance that prophets and seers fit into their descriptions of hell and the underworld. For the thousands of American and Japanese troops battling on Iwo Jima, that description matched their hellish experience on the volcanic island.

Thousands were injured, thousands died. Even more gruesome, thousands of Japanese soldiers who refused to surrender ended up buried alive, crushed when their defensive caverns collapsed under the weight of the volcanic rock or scorched to death when American troops used flame-throwers to burn them out of their positions. Their bodies were never recovered.

The Second Battalion, the Twenty-Seventh Marines, land on Iwo Jima.

According to the islanders, the spirits of those soldiers trapped under the island may want final release. Witnesses believe these ghosts are behind the most persistent paranormal problem reported since the war.

Early one morning, islander Yoshikatsu Takeda was sound asleep when a knocking at his door woke him, according to an article in the *Japan Times*, written by Nao Shimoyachi. He knew no visitor would be knocking on his door, not a living one anyway. He got out of bed, walked to the door, and opened it. As he expected, there was no one there. He called out, "Let's go home," and went back to bed.

Takeda, like hundreds of others who live on the island, says the spirits of thousands of war dead who were never properly buried visit him, looking for people to help them receive the burial they deserve. They believe these restless spirits will continue to haunt the island until they do.

How many spirits? The number could be in the thousands, according to paranormal experts familiar with Iwo Jima hauntings. Takeda said he suspects the spirits are behind the phenomena because it wasn't the first time he heard the strange knocks. The knocks occurred a couple times before, usually as he was preparing to take a flight off the island (which is now used mainly for military purposes) and back to Japan.

"I guess (the spirit) wanted me to take him over to the mainland," Takeda said. "But you need not worry. The spirits here do not hurt you."

Other witnesses stepped forward to claim that the ghosts of Iwo Jima do not just knock on doors to gain attention, they actually appear when you least expect it. Many people say they have seen the faces of the war dead in the white foam of the sea, or they will take a picture of the surf and notice what look like faces etched in the waves, faces of men wearing agonized expressions.

Soldiering On—Even After Death

Witnesses list a whole host of paranormal entities that they have encountered while staying on the solemn island of Iwo Jima, which is made especially remote because it can only be reached through military transport. As a huge military base, a number of soldiers, sailors, and Marines have written about unexplainable incidents that happened during maneuvers and training exercises on the island. According to one online forum post, for example, a Marine said his battalion had landed on the island to take part in a war game. One night, the Marines were on maneuvers, silently patrolling the hauntingly silent battleground. As they crept through the dark, dense jungle, a few of the Marines, whose senses were honed to be razor sharp by countless training missions, heard what sounded like footsteps following their platoon. In some of these war games, a group of Marines are turned into an enemy team and sent to disrupt operations. This patrol immediately guessed that one of those enemy teams was following them, perhaps preparing a sneak attack.

After gesturing to each other with hand signals—silently, so that the enemy team would not catch on to their planned counterattack—leaders selected a couple Marines to hang back as a rear guard to protect against this threat, while the rest of the column moved on toward its objective.

Curiously, nobody in the main body ever heard the commotion—shouts, firing of blanks, etc.—that would have signaled that the enemy team had been identified and repulsed. Only the uneasy sound of the ocean breeze rattled through the jungle. The main body proceeded to their objective and the team never discussed the matter.

However, one Marine who marched with the main body remained curious about the incident, so the next morning he sought out a few of the men who stood back as the rear guard positioned to engage the enemy team. When he found them, he noticed right away that something was wrong. The tough Marines turned pale white when he brought up the subject. They seemed afraid to speak, but he pestered them until they told him what happened.

According to the Marines, they dropped back and set an ambush. They caught the unmistakable sound of men walking through the jungle get louder and louder. Their fingers gripped their triggers ever tighter, expecting the enemy to come into the clearing to be greeted by the withering chatter of M 16s firing blanks. Seconds later, the enemy did appear, but it was not the enemy they expected. Instead, they could see that the soldiers following their column were Japanese soldiers, and they were not only wearing old World War II uniforms, but they were brandishing weapons from that era, too.

No word on what happened next, but the misty appearance of enemy soldiers from another time deeply affected the men, who still looked pale and didn't seem ready to talk about their run-in with the supernatural squad.

"I don't know if I fully believe them or not, but I had known them for a while, and neither was given to flights of fancy," the writer added in the online forum.

Okinawa's Restless Spirits

Historians list the amphibious invasion of the island fortress of Okinawa as one of the riskiest and most ferocious battles in the Pacific theater. The Japanese knew that the fall of the island, like a swinging gate, would clear the path for an invasion of their sacred homeland, mainland Japan. Ships that docked at Okinawa could gather fuel and supplies to encircle Japan, and bombers that used the island's airstrips could more easily reach cities and key bases in Japan.

Another battle—a psychological one—raged, as well. The Japanese military had convinced the people of the island that if the Americans landed, the invaders would surely torture and kill the inhabitants. Panic ensued among the populace when US ships appeared offshore and thousands of Marines and Army personnel spilled out of hundreds of landing craft onto the beaches. The ensuing fight racked up casualty figures that mismatched the size of the relatively small chunk of land in the Pacific. About fifty thousand Allied troops were wounded or killed, while the Japanese figure easily doubled that number.

The Americans knew they were locked in for a winner-take-all grudge match on Okinawa. Still, nothing—no amount of training or briefings from officers—could have prepared American soldiers for what happened next. A number of American troops watched, horrified, as bands of civilians ran to the edge of the island's cliffs and threw themselves into the ocean. They did so rather than risk being captured by the Americans, who had been painted as ruthless, cruel aggressors who would stop at nothing to torture and kill civilians.

The devastation of the battle and the psychic shock of the mass suicides cast a spiritual pall over the island, occult experts say, leading to numerous supernatural encounters.

Although Okinawa's people, with their traditions of ancestor and spirit worship, connected easily and deeply with notions of the supernatural, the decades since the battle saw an even greater uptick in reports of ghostly experiences. These reports don't just come from the inhabitants. The service members and their families have also said they witnessed—or became victims of—the supernatural forces that now teem on the island.

Cliff Spirits

Standing like guards along the southern coast of Okinawa are miles of formidable rocky cliffs. Staring out on the crystal blue and white-capped Pacific, the clifftop sites offer unmatched scenic views and a place for photographers to snap postcard pictures. Islanders and even a few visitors claim that the fields above the cliffs also offer a vantage spot to witness something much darker, something much more mysterious: ghosts.

There is, for example, the story of a visitor to the island who had just spent some serious, contemplative time in the Peace Museum, which rests above the rocky southern shore, the scene of so much violence and tribulation during World War II. Many comment on the sharp contrast in the space now: the serenity of the museum and the grandeur of the ocean are contrasted by the recognition that a few decades ago—just a blip in the chart of history—the very ground they now stand on had been the scene of horror and death.

Maybe those thoughts were filling the mind of this visitor as he stepped ever closer to the side of the cliffs. Maybe he imagined those gray ships and landing crafts dotting the sea in front of him. Maybe he could feel the panic of the islanders, who saw the men swarming on their beaches as vicious conquerors, not liberators.

As he got closer, though, he suddenly transitioned from imagining ghosts to actually sensing their presence. They swirled all around him.

He wasn't the only one to have this sensation. Many visitors detect something—a wind, perhaps?—rush past them toward the ocean. They claim to hear the heavy pounding of footsteps sprinting toward the cliffside, too. Some even hear shrieks. Experts on the ghosts of Okinawa believe these reports are residual spirits. In a residual haunting, the energy of highly emotionally charged events becomes embedded in the area where the event occurred. It then plays out over and over again. Sometimes these reenactments are witnessed by observers in our own reality, the theory states. Experts in the paranormal field say that the terror that the mass suicide victims must have felt certainly fits the description of an emotionally charged event.

But the paranormal incidents on the overlooks above Okinawa's southern beaches go beyond just sounds and feelings. People also claim to see the ghosts that haunt the island. Witnesses say they have seen filmy shadows streaking toward the edge of the cliffs—and then disappearing. Often, haunting screams echo over the fields as the ghosts make their appearances.

Similar apparitions are seen at a golf course on Okinawa's Kadena Air Base. According to several reports, golfers enjoying a calm, quiet evening on the links are shocked to see a group of Okinawan girls wander across the greens. Maybe they are just schoolgirls taking a shortcut, they reason. But a shortcut to where? As the golfers watch, they say the solid figures of the girls begin to fade and then finally disappear. Some of the sightings are accompanied by horrific wailing.

Experts on the base's hauntings believe the ghostly accounts are related to a World War II legend that a group of high school girls committed suicide at the very site that is now a golf course. Right before the American invasion, the Japanese military pressed the girls—some accounts say there were seventeen of them—into service. When the attack happened, the girls broke into a run and then, in one final act of desperation, committed suicide. That moment of sheer terror reportedly lives on.

More Paranormal Accounts from Kadena

Jayne Hitchcock, author of *Ghosts of Okinawa*, writes that while the whole island is supernaturally active, several spots associated with World War II actions are especially haunted. One of the most haunted sites on the island, according to her research and investigations, is a high-security area in the grassy fields of Kadena.

She writes about one famous story of a security guard who became curious about all the rumors of hauntings that swirled around the area. One spot in particular is said to be haunted by the ghosts of Japanese troops. In fact, people told him that an entire regiment of Japanese troops supposedly stalked the field. He decided to satisfy his curiosity one evening, although satisfied might not describe the result of his investigation. He said he pulled into an area and stepped out of his patrol vehicle. Immediately, he began to sense the presence of spirits. Then he heard them. The guard claimed that he was enveloped in the thunderous echo of hundreds of boots heading his way. It sounded exactly like a regiment of troops on the move. He immediately lost his nerve and jumped back into his vehicle.

Just like being caught up in the scene of a horror movie, everything seemed to go wrong. For a few paralyzing seconds that must have seemed like hours, he fumbled with his keys. Once he found the right key, the guard finally got inside the vehicle, but he couldn't get the engine started. All the while, the sounds of marching troops closed in. The guard must have had trouble determining whether it was the vibration of the marching soldiers or the rapid beating of his heart that was causing his car to shake. Finally, his car roared to life, but when he looked up, he wondered whether his efforts were in vain—a formation of Japanese soldiers with World War II–era uniforms and weapons was heading straight toward him. The grimaces and expressions on their faces did not make it look like surrender would be an option.

The guard closed his eyes. He hit the gas. And the car surged ahead—and lunged straight through the ghostly formation.

Once safely outside the clutches of the phantom Japanese regiment, he vowed never to return to that spot again.

While guards are troubled with attacking phantom regiments, maintenance workers have their own World War II spirits to battle. Hitchcock writes that there is a building that once served as a place to conduct interrogations during the war. It's essentially abandoned now. And there's a reason for that. Maintenance workers won't touch the place. They don't even like to go near it.

Witnesses claim that horrible screams emit from the building. The workers wonder whether it isn't some type of residual spirit reliving the sheer hell of an interrogation. Whatever the source, workers leave the building alone.

Sea Spirits

The island isn't the only place you'll find spirits on Okinawa; the sea that surrounds it is also allegedly filled with occult energy. And the sea-bound spirits are bent on revenge, according to some ghostly accounts.

During her stay on the island, Okinawans told Hitchcock that the ghosts of Japanese soldiers remain in the ocean, just off the coast of where the war's bloodiest fighting occurred. They also said that these soldiers may be coming back to recruit for their ghostly army. In one incident, Hitchcock writes that a group of Americans attended a party at an oceanside house. During the party, the guests noticed something absolutely bizarre. An Okinawan man who joined the party appeared to be suspended in midair over a second-floor balcony. It seemed as though he was struggling with someone who was trying to push him over the railing. But as the guests who rushed to his aid noted, no one else seemed to be nearby. It was as if an invisible force had him in its grasp. The rescuers arrived too late—just as they reached him, that force finally got the better of the man and he plummeted over the side of the balcony. The ambulance rushed the poor man to the hospital, where he remained for several days in a coma.

After hearing the strange tale of her husband's mishap, the man's wife brought in an Okinawan spirit medium, called a Yuta. The Yuta said that the spirits of Japanese soldiers who lived in the sea attacked the man. The Americans later found out that many of their neighbors were afraid of these returning Japanese warriors, according to Hitchcock. Many did not venture out late—and most never stayed out on their balconies very long after dark. I guess they did not want to be drafted into Okinawa's mysterious spirit army.

Eternal Return: The Spirits of the Philippines

Some of the most violent, brutal fighting of World War II, and perhaps in world history, occurred in the Pacific. A desperate enemy brainwashed into a "no surrender" mentality faced off against a massive well-armed American military bent on revenge. The resulting immovable object versus an unstoppable force cascaded into a conflict that covered a wide spectrum of violence—hand-to-hand combat, poundings from air to sea, and eventually highly technological weapons that created unprecedented destruction.

The fury, terror, misery, brutality, and heartbreak of the fight brewed a storm of supernatural forces that people still experience—and endure—even today, say paranormal theorists.

Witnesses have seen these ghosts of the past all over the South Pacific, in areas that the Japanese invasion forces hit the hardest during the war, as well as during American operations to claim these conquered lands and islands back from the Japanese. Few places suffered as much as the Philippines—and we will look at the occult residue from that conflict now.

Scary Seminary

During World War II, the seminary that stood on Dominican Hill was not just a spiritual refuge, it was a refuge from the onslaught of invading Japanese troops. Citizens of the Philippines hoped that they would be safe from the Japanese Imperial Army behind the walls of the seminary. They hoped that the invaders would not violate the sanctity of the church.

They were wrong.

The Japanese soldiers took the seminary over and turned the strategically important site into their headquarters. Some said that the seminary became the army's torture headquarters. The Japanese continued to face resistance from local insurgents, whom—the Japanese believed—were helping to prepare the way for an American counter-invasion. The secret police, called the Kempeitai, used the base to extract information from and exact punishment on anyone they felt might be a threat to the occupiers. Many of these suspects—along with priests, nuns, and other innocent citizens who simply ran afoul of the occupying forces—were raped, tortured, and killed at the site.

When the war ended, some of the Filipino people may have escaped the grasp of the Japanese forces, but they remained under the grasp of a spectral occupation. Dominican Hill became proof.

After extensive renovations due to the bomb damage that American forces inflicted on the site trying to recapture the base, entrepreneurs tried to turn the seminary into a hotel. They quickly found out that while they struggled to attract guests, they had no trouble marketing rooms to ghosts. Staff and visitors claimed a heartbreaking wailing came from within the corridors of the building during the day—not exactly a desirable amenity for a hotel.

At night, things get even creepier, though.

According to several reports, the ghost of a priest stalked the corridors of the building. Guests at the hotel were shocked to see an apparition gliding through the halls. Each report contained one similar gruesome detail: the ghost had no head. It is believed that the headless priest was one of the victims of Japanese secret police. There's another story that some guests reported not just seeing a headless ghost, but a headless spirit carrying a plate in his hands.

It wasn't exactly room service, though. In a final macabre twist, the plate carried a decapitated head.

Many residents who live near the site say you don't need to check in to find ghosts, either. The hill is teeming with supernatural activity, witnesses claim. Spirits of war victims—and their oppressors—are said to wander the grounds, something that continues to attract ghosthunters even today.

No one's blaming the spirits, but the hotel did not stay in operation long. The site quickly fell into disrepair and the abandoned hotel and other buildings situated where the seminary once stood soon became the center of tales of the supernatural. While the hotel industry didn't quite make a go of it on Dominican Hill, the paranormal industry made a brisk business. Hundreds of paranormal investigators—and people who just wanted a good scare—flocked to the former seminary. The abandoned hotel made the perfect living—no pun intended—lab for the researchers. And, for thrill seekers, it was almost like being placed on the set of a horror film.

Over the years, more stories—and some would say evidence—of the paranormal flooded in. People took pictures and recorded videos purported to show ghosts and other anomalous activity. The site continues to be one of the most popular spots for those looking for run-ins with the paranormal in the Philippines. But it is certainly not the only occult reminder of the war's traumatic effect on the country.

On our next stop, we will visit a World War II military complex that continues to bustle with paranormal activity.

Ghosts Haunt the Gibraltar of the East

Not all of the World War II ghosts in the Philippines are based on Dominican Hill. There was enough tragedy to go around on the island chain that became one of the war's most hotly contested pieces of real estate.

The name *Corregidor* became synonymous with the brutal, furious fighting that took place in the Philippines during World War II. With its thick walls, powerful guns, and extensive tunnel system, the island was nicknamed "The Gibraltar of the East." Japanese forces, who made relatively quick work in defeating the American and Filipino forces in the campaign to seize the country, learned a lesson in American and Filipino tenacity when they tried to crack the resistance on the island fortress. The invading Japanese forces relentlessly pounded the defenders of Corregidor. But they continued to fight.

Despite the impressive resistance, Corregidor eventually fell and became an embarrassing defeat for Douglas MacArthur, who vowed to return, even as his rescuers evacuated him from the base.

He wasn't the only one who made good on the promise to return.

Over the years since the war, more and more reports have piled up at Corregidor that indicate ghosts and spirits—

typically ghosts of soldiers involved in the bloody battle—have returned to haunt the battlefields and battle-scarred buildings.

The infamous tunnel complexes—the ones that the Japanese tried so hard to penetrate and that filled up with the dead and wounded as they tried—are probably the most haunted spots on the island, if not all of the Philippines. They sure qualify as haunted on looks alone. Long, silent, and vast, the tunnels stretch on seemingly forever under the base. If you cut the lights, the tunnels are pitch black. Visitors who tread through the underground chasms can probably imagine themselves surrounded by ghosts of battles past.

Rumors and reports of Japanese troops who committed suicide—even blowing themselves up—to avoid being captured by Allied troops also circulate among paranormal researchers, who claim that these types of incidents only increase the chances for authentic hauntings. Witnesses say they have seen lights glowing and floating down the corridors of the tunnel complex. These are, perhaps, reminders that some Japanese soldiers have not given up their posts decades later. They also say that photographers have captured this strange phenomenon, adding that it's unlikely that the glare of the tunnels' minimal lighting or other electromagnetic phenomena is creating this effect in a pitch black tunnel.

Skeptics still aren't buying the orb phenomena. They say the photographs could be the result of malfunctioning camera equipment. However, other photographers have snapped pictures that seem to show human figures lurking in the dark shadows of the facility—something much harder to explain than orbs. Some of these shots have made their way to major magazines and newspapers in the Philippines. A Filipino magazine, *People's Tonight*, published a photo that showed—according to some—the shadowy shapes of two men. One is kneeling and is turned away from the camera. It looks as though the figure is wearing a cap and uniform. Another shape looks like he is sitting on the lower deck of a bunk bed.

A psychic, who was brought in to investigate, said that the images in the pictures were spirits of Japanese soldiers who committed suicide by blowing themselves up. She believed that the ghostly images in the photos and the orbs that showed up in numerous pictures captured the form of some type of energy or power given off by the spirits.

These photos may be another piece of evidence that while General MacArthur and his American forces vowed to return to the Philippines, other forces—spiritual forces—are apparently destined to never leave.

GHOST PLANES AND
HAUNTED AIRFIELDS

When we think of ghosts, we tend to think about who: Who is haunting my house? What demon is behind the haunted activities in that building?

But in the ghost stories of World War II, you may find that it's not just people who become ghosts. These hauntings aren't always about *who*, but *what*. It turns out that things can be ghosts, too. In fact, one of the most frequently told supernatural tales about the war concerns not phantoms that are stalking the halls of an old military base, or even spirits gliding through the remains of a battlefield foxhole, but ghosts that are flying through the clouds and buzzing over fields and forests.

They're called ghost planes.

In the skies above Europe, especially the skies above the United Kingdom, witnesses have reported dozens of encounters with phantom World War II–era fighters and bombers flying overhead. These witnesses tell us that the objects aren't just little blips in the sky, but, in some cases, the planes are so close that they have seen markings and even what appear to be pilots still manning the controls. We will review some of those reports in the pages ahead.

But there's more.

As the skies buzz with haunted World War II aircraft, some ghosts are grounded. Visitors and staff members of museums that honor these mighty warbirds claim that spirits from the past may still haunt the displays, leading to bone-chilling supernatural encounters. That's up next, too.

Finally, we will explore tales of airplanes that seemed to pilot themselves during the war and ponder what forces could possibly be responsible for this.

Strap in. You're in for a bumpy flight.

The Ghost Planes of Dark Peak

With its rolling hills and patchy woodlands, you might be lulled into thinking that the last place you would encounter a supernatural force would be in the northern section of the United Kingdom's pastoral-sounding Derbyshire.

And perhaps the land itself isn't especially haunted, but the skies above the Derbyshire countryside are reportedly teeming with paranormal activity. In fact, Dark Peak, as this hilly area of Derbyshire is known, is considered the Bermuda Triangle of England. More than fifty planes have crashed there, resulting in the deaths of dozens of pilots and passengers, some of those being World War II–era fighters and bombers.

Occult experts believe those tragic accidents spawned England's weirdest spectral residue: ghost planes.

Witnesses Recount Ghost Plane Near Derbyshire

In one of the more famous examples of the ghost planes that haunt Britain's skies, witnesses have claimed to see a four-engine bomber from a bygone era lumbering across modern skies. Among those witnesses are aviation experts, who instantly recognized the distinctive sound and contours of bombers used extensively during World War II.

One couple, driving along A6 in Derbyshire—a historic road that runs north to south in the country—in the summer of 1985, looked up and saw a huge plane lumbering toward them. The first thing that the couple—Richard and Helen Jephson—noticed was how low the plane was flying. They could almost touch it, Richard told *The Derby Telegraph*.

But the weirdness did not end there.

They rolled down the windows in their vehicle and noticed that the craft made no sound, even as it cruised directly overhead, a mere few feet away. Both the husband and wife said the plane resembled the iconic Lancaster.

The plane flew so low that they were afraid it might crash. But it just sort of disappeared.

Media and law enforcement officials began to receive reports from other witnesses who also saw a similar plane and who were also worried that it was about to crash. Oddly, the sightings came from all over the countryside, not in a nice straight flight path, as one might assume would be the case if the plane was traveling toward a destination or performing in an air show, for example.

One of the witnesses just happened to be an expert on World War II aircraft. He served three years on an RAF ground crew during World War II and was looking out his bedroom window when he apparently saw the same plane that the couple watched. He gave a similar description, but added that the plane looked too small to be a Lancaster, and was more than likely an American B-24 Liberator. He added a few details—it was camouflaged and sported an antenna. Another witness, driving at the time of the sightings, confirmed he saw a low-flying plane traveling southwest during the same period, as well.

In all cases, the plane did not make a sound, even though, technically, the rumble of either a Lancaster or Liberator would have rattled the skies and probably the ground itself.

Skeptics immediately guess that the Lancaster or Liberator—whatever the case may be—was part of an air show or on its way to a historical reenactment. The reporters for *The Derby Telegraph* checked and failed to find any information about air shows or reenactments during the time of the sightings. And pilots usually don't take their four-engine World War II bombers out for unexpected joyrides, especially in the notoriously unfriendly skies above Dark Peak.

Ghost Flyer's Return Flight?

Pity the spirit world's air traffic controllers responsible for directing the busy ghostly flights above the United Kingdom.

According to paranormal theorists, another ghost fly zone exists sixty miles or so north of the Peak District. This region was the center of a ghost plane flap at the turn of the twenty-first century. And the bizarre run of weird sightings may not be over yet.

Newspaper reports suggest that the first round of phantom aircraft appearances began above the grounds of the Rolls-Royce Bankfield factory in Barnoldswick. It should be noted that although Rolls-Royce is synonymous with luxury cars, the company also built some of World War II's best aircraft engines.

On January 23, 2004, a newspaper reported that a tourist visiting Barnoldswick received an unexpected souvenir from her tour—a ghost plane sighting. The visitor said she watched as a huge gray aircraft appeared out of the mist above the Rolls-Royce factory. The plane was cruising so low that the woman and her partner thought it would crash into their car and the homes in the neighborhood for sure. But at the last second, the big plane disappeared.

They described the plane's four propellers and said the craft was huge. The most likely suspect, based on that description, would have been the Lancaster bomber, much like the one that appeared in the Peak District.

One of the witnesses, Moira Thwaites, a retired police-woman from Nelson, told the *Craven Herald*: "It was so low I fully expected it to hit us, or at least hit the houses near the Bankfield site. We both fully expected to at least hear the impact of a crash, but there was nothing. And when we both looked back there was nothing."

Trained as a police officer to be careful when observing details, she described the huge plane, saying it had a full set of propellers slashing through wind; however, she was shocked that the plane was absolutely silent. She couldn't hear a thing.

"Whatever it was had vanished," she said. "There wasn't a sound from the engine at all. It was really weird, but we both know what we saw and I just wondered if anyone else had reported seeing anything."

That call for other witnesses was quickly answered, Donald Cooper, an expert on aerial phenomena, told the newspaper. Cooper, the president of the Skipton research society, SERIUS—which investigates the anomalous happenings in the Yorkshire area—soon received a flood of new reports and details. All of the reports corroborated the description of the plane that flew over the Rolls-Royce factory. Witnesses described it as a big plane—a propeller-driven gray bomber—that, despite its size, moved silently across the sky. Interestingly, but typical in ghost plane sightings, these reports came from all over the area and not simply from spots along a direct flight path.

"I must have taken 30 or more calls since Friday from a variety of people ranging from professionals to members of the public, councillors to pub landlords," said Cooper.

The article also states: "Some have even come forward saying they saw something of that description several years ago. In particular one elderly gentleman rang to say he had seen the plane the article referred to. He also said there used to be an old airfield at Greenberfield Lane (in Barnoldswick) which I didn't know about. Coincidentally, Mr. Cooper pointed out that an article had also appeared in a national newspaper last Friday about 'time slips,' which said there had been many reports of people claiming to have seen World War Two aircraft as if re-running missions, often silently, from 60 years before."

"I Know What They Look Like"

For two years, the skies—and the interdimensional doorways—above Barnoldswick remained quiet and ghost plane free. A phone call to the *Craven Herald* on February 24, 2006, ended all that. The caller—a seventy-year-old Skipton resident—told a reporter that he saw a bomber that looked exactly like the one that scared the area a few years before. The plane was flying low—at about four hundred feet off the ground—toward a field that was once supposedly used as an emergency landing strip during World War II.

This time there was no mistaking the type of aircraft. It was a Lanc. The witness, who asked the reporter to keep his name out of the paper, was alive during World War II and saw many Lancasters.

Skeptics floated several theories. They suggested that the witness misidentified modern aircraft, such as one of the big propeller-driven Hercules craft that Royal Air Force (RAF) pilots may have been flying during military exercises.

The witness was adamant, however. He knew exactly what he saw.

"I saw them during the war so I know what they look like—this wasn't a modern plane," the man told the reporter, referring to the distinctive bomber.

Hercules aircraft are vastly different from a Lancaster, according to Cooper, who implied that the difference would be recognized by someone who was familiar with the World War II warbird. He added that the modern RAF does not allow planes to fly at such a low altitude, especially in a relatively populated area.

Cooper said it wasn't just the quality of the description of the phantom aircraft that made the sighting impressive, it was the quality of the witness.

"I'm keeping an open mind, but I have to believe the witnesses who all seem to be balanced, professional people and not people coming out of the pub after one too many," he said.

America's Ghost Plane Incidents

On the morning of December 7, 1941, most of the people in California went about their normal routine, blissfully unaware that the first bombs of World War II had already started to drop on American soil and that thousands of American sailors and airmen found themselves caught up in a slaughter. They had no idea that the war had come, perhaps not to America's front door, but certainly to its front gate.

While many Californians were oblivious, a few others in the state received an early warning that something was amiss. A number of these witnesses later recounted that while outside on what seemed to be a normal early December morning, they saw an unusual sight in the sky. Flying low across the horizon was a warplane, which sputtered and twisted and appeared to be in considerable distress. More ominously, smoke gushed out of the engine as the plane seemed to lose altitude. If they didn't know better, the witnesses would have said that the plane had been the victim of some sort of an attack. Witnesses gasped as the plane flew out of sight. Some claimed that crash sounds—the crunch of metal and the concussion of explosions—echoed through the area.

They alerted authorities and soon a convoy of police, fire, and emergency vehicles were roaring into the forest, toward where the witnesses said they saw the plane crash. As they drove, the sheriff must have thought they were being dragged into a wild goose chase. Deeper and deeper into the dense forest they ventured, with no sign of a crashed plane, or even a crash site. Surely there would be burnt brush, or trees shorn off by the speeding aircraft. But they couldn't find a single bit of evidence that a plane ever crashed. Nobody considered the people who reported the crash to be your typical small-town nuts who might get some sort of cheap thrill out of a hoax. The witnesses included some of the area's most prominent and trusted citizens.

Eventually, the team turned around. As the members did, they probably switched the radios from frequencies used by emergency crews to commercial radio. The airwaves were already filled with news reports and special updates explaining the attack on Pearl Harbor. The nation was at war. Some people put two and two together and arrived at a disturbing conclusion. An air attack on US forces at the exact same time as the appearance of a heavily damaged US fighter plane? It was more than a coincidence.

But people who suggested such a weird explanation had to contend with some significant details. California is far from Pearl Harbor, way outside the range of the typical fighter plane of that era. Also, American forces in the

Pacific had barely mustered any sort of aerial resistance to the marauding Japanese planes.

Some experts offer another theory: US planes were aloft during the fight at Pearl Harbor and, though vastly out-numbered, fought bravely against the Japanese pilots. Historians say that at least five American pilots managed to get their planes in the air. A group of American pilots chased off a group of bombers preparing to attack an airfield. An aerial melee ensued. One American pilot was pulling his P-36 fighter behind an enemy bomber, just about to squeeze the trigger, when a Japanese pilot pulled in behind the US fighter. The bullets ripped through the American's plane and it began to smoke.

Another American joined in and, based on reports, all four planes plummeted into steep dives. Only one American pilot—Lewis Sterling, the end of the formation—could pull out of the dive and survive the fight.

There are those who now question the appearance of the ghostly plane over California during the initial moments of World War II. Could this bizarre sighting be related to the American pilot who was shot down off the coast of Hawaii? The description of the plane resembles the single prop P-36 flown by US forces. The amount of damage suffered by the plane, as reported by the surviving witness, also matches the ghost plane.

Did the pilot somehow make it out of the crash and manage, against all probability, to maneuver his plane back to the mainland? Or could it be that these prominent citizens of California saw a ghostly apparition of the pilot and his stricken plane, a bizarre aerial reenactment of one of America's darkest, yet most heroic, moments?

Mistaken Identity?

Skeptics say that this story is nothing more than folklore that grew out of a better documented air crash a year later. These skeptics suggest that people who refer to the Pearl Harbor ghost plane are actually referring to an incident that began December 8, 1942, not December 7, 1941. However, even that 1942 incident is wrapped in mystery, as we will see.

Sources indicate that the strange event began on a quiet evening in December of 1942. The skies were overcast. For Californians, a year of war footing dissipated a lot of the panic that gripped the coast after the Japanese easily blasted their way through the country's prized naval base. But a watchful wariness remained.

A group of radar operators scanned their scopes, part of that watchful wariness. That evening, they noticed something strange on their radar scopes. A blip appeared in the eastern edge of the screen that seemed to represent an aircraft heading toward the American coast. They scrambled two fighters to meet the threat.

*A group of children look at a Curtiss
P-40 Advanced Pursuit plane.*

As the planes bore down on the bogey, they replied to the radar team that it didn't resemble a Japanese plane heading toward the coast; it looked more like a United States P-40 fighter plane. The radar team could hear the surprise and distress in the voice of one of the pilots as he radioed back that the plane was considerably shot up.

There was another issue: the plane had strange markings. The markings on the plane were old—in fact, these markings hadn't appeared on an American aircraft since the attack on Pearl Harbor.

Zooming in closer to try to make visual contact with the pilot, they then noticed that the landing gear had been blown away. How did a plane take off without landing gear? The pilots were mystified. The ghost plane's pilot was obviously injured. When he saw friendly aircraft next to him, the pilot of the stricken craft smiled and waved slightly. The damaged craft then banked and screamed toward the ground.

Helplessly, the interceptor pilots watched the P-40 crash into the ground.

Officials organized a search team and headed toward the crash site. Unlike our previous story, the rescuers did find the crashed plane. But they didn't find the pilot. He had—somehow—disappeared. The pilot did, however, leave a diary that managed to survive the fiery crash. According to the pilot's handwritten notes, he was stranded on Mindanao, an island about 1,300 miles away. But the pilot never mentioned how he got to the desolate island. Perhaps he was shot down on the island and somehow found a way to repair his plane well enough to take off, some people speculate. But critics say that getting a heavy P-40 airborne without landing gear baffles the imagination. The odds would be stacked against that.

But for American airmen who faced the brutal odds of beating back the Japanese empire in those dark days following Pearl Harbor, they say overcoming massive challenges and long odds wasn't impossible. It was just another day's work.

The Phantom Flying Fortress

Out on the perimeter of the air base in Belgium, the keen-eyed antiaircraft gun crew, squatting down in the sand-bag-filled ditch in the middle of a grassy field, scanned the horizon for any sign of German planes. The rumble of aircraft engines caused the men to stir. A sizzle of nervous energy pulsed along the spines of the newer gunners, but the older vets could tell just by the sound of the incoming aircraft that it was one of theirs. It was a friendly. And, sure enough, the black dot on the horizon gradually became a silhouette and then took the shape of an American B-17 bomber. The newbies must have breathed a sigh of relief as the warbird, wheels down, perfectly maneuvered into position to land.

From their vantage point—a brown hole in the ground among the pock-marked grassy plain—the gun crew watched the bomber make a perfect landing and roll to the edge of the tarmac, just as inbound planes normally do. It bounced a couple times as it drew closer to their position, and then one wing dipped into the ground. That's when the gun crew began to murmur. Is everything okay? Was this an emergency landing? The plane eventually stopped just a few yards from their gun position.

Once the plane made this abrupt, unconventional stop, the base personnel noticed something strange, too. For starters, the bomber crew didn't exit the B-17. If the crew had experienced problems aboard the plane, some type of emergency, the spectators saw no sign of any urgency from the crew. And the threat of a fuel explosion at the very least would prompt crews to rush out of the plane as soon as they could. In fact, they were trained to do just that. However, the crew did not open the doors and hatches to escape. No ladders dropped from the openings. The bomber just sat there, puttering at the end of the runway.

Emergency crews rushed to the scene. As they closed in, they did not see any signs of battle damage. Initially, they theorized that if gunfire raked the plane, injuring but not killing the crew, maybe the weakened crew managed to pilot the crippled craft back to base. One problem existed with that theory: they couldn't see any obvious battle damage.

If the mystery was deep when the emergency crews examined the outside of the plane, things downright cratered as they cautiously entered the bomber. There was no sign of the ten or so men who crewed the massive B-17—no pilot, no co-pilot, no gunners, no navigator, no bombardier. Weirder still, no signs of any type of trauma could be found inside the plane, either—no blood, no tissue, and no injured bodies.

Somehow, a completely pilotless complex flying fortress—a plane that takes hundreds of hours to learn how to fly and hundreds more to learn how to operate as a team—had flown and, more mind-bogglingly, completed a complex landing maneuver without a pilot or crew.

They immediately called an investigator. The officer in charge of the investigation—a major—was more shocked than the first responders. He saw that nearly everything was intact. The navigator's logs still sat there undisturbed. He apparently scrawled a single entry on the log: "Bad Flak."

The following comes from the report that the major finally compiled about the incident: "We now made a thorough search and our most remarkable find in the fuselage was about a dozen parachutes neatly wrapped and ready for clipping on. This made the whereabouts of the crew even more mysterious. The Sperry bombsight remained in the Perspex nose, quite undamaged, with its cover neatly folded beside it. Back on the navigator's desk was the code book giving the colors and letters of the day for identification purposes. Various fur-lined flying jackets lay in the fuselage together with a few bars of chocolate, partly consumed in some cases."

The near-perfect condition of the craft allowed the investigator to track down where the plane flew from and a weird story began to emerge. Based on the information he uncovered, the plane was part of a mission to bomb targets at the Merseburg oil complex. The mission for this bomber seemed doomed from the beginning. It could barely keep up with the rest of the bomber fleet, then the bomb rack malfunctioned and they could not jettison their load, which increased the struggle of the aircraft to maintain its speed and stay in formation.

A B-17 all alone in the sky would be an easy target for a prowling Nazi pilot, for sure.

Antiaircraft crews in the heavily protected Merseburg area zeroed in on the slower and lower bomber. One shot of flak knocked out the number three engine and another one hit the bomb bay door. With all the munitions still there, the crew considered it a mystery that the whole plane did not blow up.

Limping back to England would not be in the cards, the pilot realized. His goal was to keep the crew safe and make sure the bomber did not fall into enemy hands. He swung the big bird toward Allied-controlled Belgium and ordered the crew to bail out. (The investigators would later learn that the crew survived and were rescued.)

From this point, however, the investigator could only speculate that some sort of miracle occurred after the crew abandoned their wounded ship. The malfunctioning engines must have restarted. The landing gear must have come on. The automatic pilot, set by the actual pilot, must have maneuvered the plane along a trajectory toward the RAF air base and set it—nearly perfectly—on the ground.

Another mystery continues to be debated. Why were there still parachutes in the craft? Perhaps the crew just carried some extra ones, or brought along empty parachute packs, the investigator shrugged.

This account of the phantom flying fortress may actually be just one of several reports of planes that piloted themselves during the war. Aviation experts say that aeronautical engineers designed these birds to fly and they kept flying even when people abandoned them. Others, those with a more metaphysical bent, believe that this never-say-die B-17 could never have "piloted" itself into a landing. They say that this bomber, as well as the other warbirds that managed to take care of themselves without a crew, are piloted by spirit forces who bring them safely to the ground.

Haunted Bases and Airfields

If the skies are crowded with ghost planes, you are probably guessing that the air bases that served an important role in waging the air war in World War II have their own supernatural legacy. And you would be guessing exactly right.

Occult experts consider World War II–era air bases and airfields—some of them still in use and some of them abandoned—extremely haunted locations. As we'll find out in the pages ahead, some of the hauntings are anchored in certain buildings, particularly buildings with a history of violence, death, and mayhem. These stories can also swirl around certain personalities, such as a soldier who lost his life in the fight during the great war.

Haunts in Hawaii—Hickam Air Force Base

Pearl Harbor is arguably the most haunted piece of property on the Hawaiian Islands. Ghosts haunt the *Arizona* Memorial and the harbor itself, as you will read. But the harbor isn't the only spot hit by the Japanese attack—and it isn't the only spot for ongoing supernatural attacks. One of the key objectives of the Japanese bombing runs—Oahu's Hickam Air Base—is also a target of paranormal activity, according to numerous witnesses who have served at or visited the base.

Numbers vary, but most records suggest about one hundred ninety people died in the attack on Hickam. Most paranormal theorists suggest that the damage, death, and tragedy increases the likelihood of supernatural encounters.

And, indeed, there seems to be a long history of ghost stories and ghostlore here that stretches back to that pivotal first moment of World War II. Some of these stories come from the many service members who lived in, worked on, and guarded the base.

In our first story, an air force security specialist said one shift in a building rumored to be the most haunted property on the base was enough to convince him of the base's paranormal legacy. The specialist wrote on the Your Ghost Stories website that he was assigned to work in the 12th Air Force headquarters building, which, according to his sources, served as a temporary morgue right after the 1941 attack.

On the first shift, at three a.m.—a typical time for paranormal activity to occur, it should be noted—the building seemed to come alive. Alarms started to ring out. The highly sensitive motion sensors began to detect presences and a "special response team" (SRT) came in to investigate. Our witness decided he would follow along with the SRT as backup. He noticed that everyone seemed a bit on edge, and for a bunch of guys who trained each day to take on any security challenge, this struck him as odd.

Another aspect of the operation stood out to him: Even as a trainee, he knew that the team should clear the building—go through room by room and ensure the building is secure. Protocol required that they check every nook and corner of a building when looking for possible intruders. But this SRT was in no hurry to investigate. They just walked directly to the alarm control panel and shut it off, then entered the incident in their log.

When the witness traveled back to his headquarters, he asked his training officer—a sergeant—about the incident and why the team didn't bother clearing the building. The answer surprised him, but at least it prepared him for the remaining days of his paranormal adventure while stationed at Hickam. The officer explained that the alarm routinely sounded between three and three thirty a.m. Even though the system was checked and rechecked and no mechanical problems were found, the alarm continued to be triggered by some unknown, unseen force. For most of the officers who experienced it—and we're talking about some cold, skeptical, evidence-seeking investigators—the cause could only be described as anomalous. Or paranormal.

The sergeant revealed another insight. He asked his subordinate if he ever wondered why there was a guard shack posted outside of the building. Normally guards are posted inside the building.

New to the base, the airman never even considered that the guard shack was out of place until the sergeant called it to his attention during their conversation. Then the light went on—the sergeant was right. CQ desks—or Charge of Quarters desks—are universally placed inside the building. Usually, the desks must be staffed twenty-four hours a day to monitor traffic coming in and out of the facility.

Indeed, on further reflection, it was definitely weird that the guards sat outside this building and not any of the other barracks on the base. Before the airman could answer, his training officer filled him in on the alleged reason.

They moved the guards outside the building because the strange activity inside the building was just too weird and disconcerting, the sergeant explained. In fact, it defeated the purpose of stationing guards in the facility when the events they experienced in the building continually distracted the guards and had them on edge. The officer read a list of reports that had triggered officials to move the CQ desk. Some guards said they could hear people walking down the halls. When they went to confront the intruders, they found no signs of life in the empty halls. They even heard people talking when the building theoretically should have been deserted. The audible sensations were nothing. Other people reported smelling a horrendous scent, like rotting flesh. For some soldiers, it could be just a weird and uncomfortable annoyance, but for witnesses who knew about the facility's role as a morgue and hospital during the Pearl Harbor attack, the smell was deeply disturbing.

A set of stairs in the building would also shake uncontrollably, almost as if some heavy yet invisible weight was rapidly pressing down on them. It probably wasn't hard for those who experienced this phenomenon to imagine it as mimicking the effect of soldiers, sailors, and rescue workers running up and down those stairs, trying to save the lives of the wounded by bringing them out of harm's way during the battle.

According to the guard, the spirits wasted no time before introducing themselves to him. On his first shift, the witness experienced the full range of paranormal activity that his sergeant briefed him on. The sounds of people talking and walking and the sounds of soldiers rushing up and down the stairs crackled throughout the night. And, of course, at 3:17 a.m., during his first shift, the motion detector rang out—signaling presences on both the basement level and the third floor. At the same time! Maybe the equipment malfunctioned—but for two separate alarms to sound at the same time would be quite a coincidence. He looked for intruders, but he knew, deep down, that since the building had been secured at five p.m. the previous afternoon, he wouldn't find anyone—anyone living, that is.

His check confirmed that intuition. There was no one anywhere near the building at that time of night, let alone in it.

The incident became just the first of many to be added to the guard's list of strange encounters during his time at Hickam.

Guard dogs—not creatures known to back down from their duties—often refused to enter the building, or would only do so only with great coaxing from their handlers. They would whimper and growl, or hide behind their handler, this security officer said.

He also noticed that on other bases, soldiers and airmen regularly returned to their offices to catch up on work at night. Not here. After five p.m., the building stood vacant. After a while, though, this guard got it. Even some of America's bravest service members considered it an "unnerving place to work."

This security specialist joined dozens of others who experienced inexplicable events at Hickam. Some report seeing water faucets turning on and off by themselves. Others have seen weird glowing shapes walking through the halls and up and down the steps. Some of those witnesses who came to Hickam, came either as skeptics or were simply indifferent to or ignorant about paranormal powers, but they walked away—or marched away—total believers.

Schofield Barracks: Target of Ghostly Attacks

At the time of the attack on Pearl Harbor, Schofield Barracks was home to two newly formed Army divisions—the 24th and 25th. On December 7, 1941, the military base found itself in the sights of Japanese pilots. The base's proximity to Wheeler Army Airfield made the barracks a tempting target for strafing Japanese planes and the unintended target of bombs that were meant for the airfield. Schofield became another grisly scene of destruction and carnage. Like Hickam and other places in Pearl Harbor, it's now the site of paranormal events.

One woman submitted her paranormal encounter to the Army Wife 101 website. She said she had a direct encounter with a full-bodied apparition of one of those martial spirits. According to her tale, she was house-sitting for her brother while he was deployed in Iraq. Almost immediately, the woman detected something amiss in the home. Doors would unexpectedly slam shut and she couldn't find any natural explanation, like a draft or a faulty hinge. Then, the television began to turn on and off by itself. Maybe it was a broken remote control, or perhaps the neighbor's control was interfering with her television?

But the activity escalated.

She said she went to bed one night, keeping her door open so that she could hear her young daughter, who slept in the next room. Suddenly, the house sitter woke up at exactly 3:31 a.m. Make sure you remember that time from our other stories of Pearl Harbor spirits. She remembered the exact time because what happened next so deeply disturbed her that the time was etched in her memory. And it wasn't so much when she woke up, but how she woke up that was even more disturbing.

A raspy voice echoed through the room, according to the witness. Boom! She sat up and looked toward the door. Standing in the entryway was a soldier decked out in World War II–era gear.

"Get out!" the soldier told her.

Once the initial shock disappeared, and despite the command, the woman said she did not fear the apparition. She was what she termed an "empath"—someone who could sense the emotions or mental states of another person, even a dead person. In the paranormal community, the powers of an empath are said to extend beyond the ability to connect with living beings, but also to those who have passed on. The woman must have sensed that the spirit was not there to frighten her out of her brother's house, but possibly to warn her. Maybe, this was the spirit reliving the Pearl Harbor attack. If so, his command to get out may have been more of a command to seek safety and avoid the bombs that were falling on the base.

In any case, the woman and the spirit had an old-fashioned stare down. She refused to budge and eventually told the soldier spirit, "I am not leaving. This is my house!"

As soon as she took this stand, the spirit disappeared. When he did, both her bedroom door and the door of the room her daughter was sleeping in slammed shut simultaneously.

The spirit vanished. But for this resident of Schofield base—as well as dozens of other witnesses to Pearl Harbor's paranormal legacy—the ghosts and spirits who remained after the vicious attack on United States soil may vanish temporarily, but they will never disappear entirely.

Spectral Displays at the National Museum of the United States Air Force

If checking out some official displays of America's World War II aerial might is on your historic "must-see list," you will probably want to travel to Wright-Patterson Airfield and visit the National Museum of the United States Air Force.

And, it just so happens that if you want a chance to see the *spectral* might of World War II warbirds, Wright-Patterson, near Dayton, Ohio, is the place to be too. At least, many workers and visitors say it's the most haunted military museum in the United States. It may be the most haunted museum period. People have witnessed the whole nine yards of supernatural happenings there, including an oft-repeated tale that apparitions of pilots continue to appear at the controls of their aircrafts, and also stalk the museum's halls.

The paranormal activity seems to center on a few of the aircraft on display, and the World War II planes in particular.

As you might expect, the big bombers that unleashed the most amount of damage on the enemies seem to be the most haunted.

The Liberator's Mission Isn't Over Yet

The B-24 Liberators on display at the museum are among the best-loved exhibits. The museum has at least two of the bombers that became famous for their long-range attacks during the war, including those on the Ploesti oil fields in Romania, where Nazi forces received most of the oil to fuel their war machine.

And they're both haunted. The displays are so popular because of the stories attached to the warbirds—some of which are ghost stories. One Liberator, nicknamed the Strawberry Bitch (which probably doesn't hurt its popularity among visitors) has a haunted reputation that's just as saucy as its moniker and pinup nose art suggests. In fact, it might be the pinup girl immortalized on the plane's surface who is behind some of the more aggressive paranormal strikes against men trying to get fresh with her. Some witnesses have the marks and scars to prove it.

With its extended range, the Liberator was ideal for missions over vast stretches of the Pacific, too. However, the Strawberry Bitch, one of more than 18,000 Liberators that the United States produced, flew in combat missions over the deserts of North Africa during 1943 and 1944. In 1959, pilots flew her to the museum. The tales of ghostly activity began soon after that.

B-24 Liberators are seen flying over Romania in 1944.

For example, people say as they approached the display they could see a strange light moving around in the craft. According to other reports, the entire interior of the plane seemed to illuminate with a soft glow. Debunkers quickly surmised that the effects were related to subtle changes in lighting. Staff and visitors, however, said they witnessed things that had nothing to do with lighting. They heard rattles and clanks in the gunner's undercarriage. When the witnesses checked to find out who was making the racket, there was nobody there.

The spirit makes its presence known in much more physical ways. One worker made the following startling claim. He said that he was working the night shift. The shift was nice and quiet, typically. But something about the quiet unnerved him and that made this shift not so nice. Most of the workers say that there is something unsettling about the silence in the museum at night, almost like the paranormal powers at work in the facility are building up their energy.

In this case, the man did not have to wait long for that power to manifest during the night shift.

The janitor said while working near the Strawberry Bitch he sensed a presence. Then, out of nowhere, he felt the sharp sting of a wicked slap across his face. Wildly, he spun around and around, trying to locate the source of the blow, but couldn't find it. There were no noises, like the sounds of the footsteps of a pranking coworker making a hasty retreat from the scene of the crime.

All alone, with only silence and fear as his constant companions now, the janitor was forced to contemplate the stinging encounter with the supernatural. There are no clues to what precipitated the attack—maybe the spirit of the saucy nose art pinup did not like being stared at. And there is no word on how long the janitor stayed on the staff of the museum. An attack like that could make you rethink your career choices.

But the janitor wasn't the only witness who was on the receiving end of some paranormal punishment. A group of women who were part of the night cleaning crew said that some force attacked them. They claimed that someone—or something—pulled their hair whenever they were in the plane. Sometimes, the ladies claimed they didn't even need to climb aboard to suffer abuse. They say if they even got close to the Strawberry Bitch they would sometimes feel a force pull their hair.

Lady Be Cursed?

Another B-24D with parts on display at the museum is the Lady Be Good. It, too, has a cursed reputation. The plane is named after one of the most famous stories of World War II resilience—and tragedy. Official records for the 376th Bombardment Group (Heavy) indicate that the nine-man crew of the brand-new Lady Be Good was part of an operation that would include twenty-five B-24s based in Libya. Their mission was to bomb the Naples harbor.

The Lady Be Good took off with orders to swoop in with the second wave of thirteen B-24s and release its bombs over the harbor. This was the first time the crew flew together, but there was no such thing as beginner's luck for the crew. The mission seemed cursed from the start. As soon as the Lady Be Good lifted off the runway a desert sandstorm erupted. Poor visibility meant that the plane could not join the rest of the bomber formation. Some of the planes returned back to base. The new crew of the Lady Be Good trudged on, deciding to attack the target alone, if necessary.

More bad luck hit, though. Clouds and bad weather obscured the primary target. The planes that did make it to Naples proceeded to a secondary target; others ditched their payload of bombs into the Mediterranean so they could make it back to base with fuel to spare.

Although there is some debate about what happened next, most historians suggest that the Lady Be Good's bad luck took a fatal turn. Alone and plagued by the bad weather that hit the region, the bomber drifted over the base and into the vast desert. For all intents and purposes, the plane disappeared; or, rather, it seemed as if the bomber was swallowed up by the desert.

It wasn't until sixteen years later that a group of British archeologists spotted the Lady Be Good while flying over the area. Most of the bodies were recovered. They found one airman's body a hundred miles from the crash site, obviously on a journey to find help for the stranded crew.

The plane itself, of course, sustained damage beyond repair. But, many of the plane's parts—despite the years of exposure to the intense desert sun and wicked sand storms—were found to be operable and were installed in other planes. The Lady Be Good's bad luck followed.

One plane with the Lady Be Good's transmitters had to ditch its cargo before making an emergency landing, sources say. A C-47 with a radio receiver from the bomber crashed into the Mediterranean and a plane with the Lady Be Good's armrest also crashed.

Workers in the museum say that there are a few pieces of memorabilia that were returned from the Lady Be Good's crash site and displayed at the museum. They notice that the parts are often moved, though everyone swears they didn't touch the display.

There are other signs that the display is haunted. Similar to paranormal activity near the other museum relics, unusual lights appear to turn on and off and drift around the Lady Be Good exhibit. Other people will rush to the nearest staff member on duty and swear they just saw—out of the corners of their eyes—pilots walking around the display. Then, when they turned to check out who the guests—or intruders—were, they couldn't find a soul, so to speak. They had simply disappeared.

These are all signs, according to paranormal theorists, that the misfortunate Lady Be Good is still restless.

Does a Victim's Spirit Still Linger?

"Bockscar," a majestic B-29 that now rests in the museum, effectively ended World War II when it dropped the last atomic bomb of the war on the Japanese city of Nagasaki. Named after the plane's pilot, Frederick Bock, Bockscar's new mission seems aimed at ending skepticism of the museum's haunted reputation.

Haunted activity began almost as soon as the B-29 was brought to the museum, but the haunting has a twist. It's not a former crew member who is apparently behind the paranormal activity that surrounds the bomber; it's one of its victims. Night security guards claim that they've seen an apparition of a young Japanese boy near the display. They say the boy darts around the plane and then runs under the aircraft where he hides, or disappears. Many believe that the boy is one of the victims of the Bockscar's historic war-ending bombing run; others say it's just a kid who loves playing near the big bomber. And skeptics say it's just a matter of overactive imaginations.

Other Signs

While the bombers seem to attract all of the supernatural attention, other witnesses report that activity occurs all up and down the long corridors and expansive display lobbies in the museum. According to various reports of employees, the planes—even though many are weighed down with cement to keep them in place—are often moved. Other people, especially folks who are in the building after closing hours, say they hear whispering. Occasionally, metallic clangs unexpectedly burst out and echo through the facility. It sounds like airplane pieces crashing to the ground.

Just an accident, possibly.

But others have noticed a pattern to it. The noises remind them of a crew working to repair an old warbird. It's hard for them to blame the event just on random building noises.

And with the museum's haunted reputation, it's easy for museum-goers to believe that the sounds of the phantom aircrew may be just one more clue that could unravel in the mystery of the National Museum of the United States Air Force.

The Haunted Bomber of Cosford Aerospace Museum

Two engineers gathered under the wing of the once proud warbird—resting somewhat dejectedly in the Albrighton, UK, Cosford Aerospace Museum in 1979—and surveyed the task before them. It wasn't going to be easy. But the mechanics and World War II aircraft restoration buffs gazing over the remains of the plane swore they would turn the pitiful heap of metal, wire, hydraulics, and rubber back into the once mighty Avro Lincoln heavy bomber that first cast the sweeping shadow of its 120-foot wingspan along the tarmac during the final days of World War II.

As the one engineer climbed into the cockpit to make repairs there, the other stood under the wing. Out of the corner of his eyes, he saw a man approach. He walked smartly and with a definite sense of purpose toward the worker, like he knew exactly where he was going. He attracted the attention of the worker. But something seemed strange about their guest. First, the two workers in the plane were the only people supposed to be in the hangar at the time. It got stranger, though. To the amazement—or perhaps the horror—of the engineer, the stranger gradually faded out of existence with each step, until he completely disappeared.

Blown away by what he just saw, the man called to his coworker, who had busied himself making repairs in the cockpit. Unfortunately, he saw nothing. There's no word about this engineer's reaction to his colleague's run-in with this specter, but you wouldn't fault the guy for assuming his friend may have been whiffing too much aviation fluid that day. But, the next morning, both workers received a sign that the supernatural sighting wasn't caused by fumes, but by a phantom. The two men reported that they arrived at work the next morning and instantly noticed something amiss. Someone had placed rows of aircraft parts and tools, perfectly aligned, underneath the bomber's massive fuselage. They wondered, could someone else be repairing the plane? But they knew of no one else who was scheduled to work on the aircraft, and they had stayed late enough the night before to know that they were the last ones to exit the building. After this incident, skepticism was tossed aside, and from that point forward, both mechanics believed that a ghost was haunting the building—and perhaps the bomber itself.

Paranormal Parachute?

One electrician says he isn't sure there's a ghost that haunts the hangar. His encounter, which is better placed on the miraculous interventions list, makes him think the supernatural force may be an angel. At least he or she acts like one at times. According to his account, he was about fifteen feet off of the floor when he lost his balance and started to fall. A few years earlier, he had a similar fall from an airplane and the mishap left him with an injured spine. As he plummeted toward the floor, he recalled thinking, "This is it." This fall might damage his spine even more or kill him.

But then something amazing happened. The electrician said as he winced, preparing for the inevitable pain from slamming into the concrete floor, his momentum slowed and he felt like he was floating. He slowly and gently landed on the floor, as if an invisible force had prevented a fatal fall.

It would seem fitting for the ghost of an airman to serve as a paranormal parachute and cushion the fall of a man who worked to restore the old warbirds in the hangar.

The incidents continued over the next few years. In 1980, in fact, a staff member was closing up shop when he thought he saw a shadow move toward the bomber. He hit the lights and searched for the intruder, but the hangar stood empty. So he turned off the lights again and instantly the "cloudy thing" was there by the plane again.

More reports began to come in, not just from staff, but visitors, too. Several people said they saw a man dressed as an airman straight out of a World War II newsreel. He looked like he was ready to take off for a bombing run. Others said they thought they saw someone in the clear bubble—or observation dome—of the aircraft. The figure in the dome wasn't just a visitor trying to stow away in the plane. This man wore a flying helmet. People also experienced and documented classic paranormal phenomena—drastic temperature shifts, the sound of footsteps, and more—over the years.

For most who have experienced the haunting of the hangar, the question isn't *is* the hangar haunted, it's *who or what* is haunting it. And everyone has their own list of likely spirit suspects. Some believe a long-dead pilot is behind the supernatural activity. Descriptions of the apparitions give credence to the notion that this is an airman lost in battle, they add. For example, in 1980 a visitor saw a "fair haired man in a white polo neck sweater [sic] and forage cap" in the plane's cockpit. Four years later, a man who looked a lot like the dapper ghost sitting in the cockpit was seen by a television camera operator for BBC. The television crew was in the hangar reporting on—you guessed it—the spooky goings-on at the airfield. They didn't just catch a quick glimpse of the ghost; they reportedly recorded a bunch of scary sounds during their investigation, too.

But there is one problem with the ghost pilot theory. No one has evidence that a pilot died on that bomber. But champions of this theory are quick to add that it could just be a ghost attached to the airport who likes to hang out near the old bomber.

One guess, mentioned in the BBC documentary, is that a pilot named Hiller may be the spirit responsible for the haunting. However, as author Neil Arnold discussed in his book *Shadows in the Sky: The Haunted Airways of Britain*, there are many who believe the haunting has multiple sources. Hiller reportedly was the last person to pilot this particular Avro Lincoln. He did not die in it. However, when he landed the craft after her last flight he did say that he loved the plane so much that he'd come back to haunt it. Many years later, the theory goes, Hiller died and fulfilled this promise.

A whole other group of paranormal theorists suggest that the ghost is the spirit of an aircraft mechanic, or just someone who loves planes. Those who back this theory have some proof. According to one tale, a mechanic was making some repairs under the belly of the big Avro and dropped his wrench. He began to feel around for the tool, but couldn't locate it. Without warning, someone "thrust" the wrench into his hand. The mechanic was shocked initially, but after this surprise settled, he became convinced that this helpful specter knew a thing or two about repairs.

Haunting or Hoaxing

Just when everyone started to suspect that the activity at the airfield absolutely had a supernatural origin, the BBC uncovered some startling new evidence. The documentary reported that a few of the engineers who claimed that they witnessed the ghost actually engineered nothing more than an elaborate hoax. According to this story, they heard that the Avro was going to be transferred to a new museum and they had grown attached to it, so they dreamed up the spooky activity and poltergeist effects to increase attention to the display and hopefully stop the move.

However, paranormal believers counter that more and more people were experiencing unusual activity at the museum, not just a few sketchy engineers. In fact, after the BBC documentary hit the airwaves and more accounts of the supernatural began to circulate, the airfield was inundated with ghosthunting groups and crowds of people hoping to catch sight of the phantom flyer. And lots apparently did. Those ghosthunters also reportedly captured evidence from EVPs, including engines rumbling, people talking, and a range of other auditory evidence. But the rush of supernatural faithful also caused some problems—especially safety and security issues—for the airfield. They decided, at least for a time, to ground the ghosthunting groups.

In light of the reports that people faked at least some of the accounts and evidence, a group of paranormal proponents put forth yet one more argument: the activity is fake *and* real. This theory is that the spirit that haunts the museum is a tulpa, or a mind-created spirit. Paranormal researchers often refer to the Philip Experiment as an example of this type of haunting. In the 1970s, a group of parapsychologists meditated on details of a fictional character named Philip. Then they tried to contact him. Soon enough, this "ghost" reached out to the group, knocking on the table to give them answers to questions and moving objects on demand. The members said that Philip eventually freed itself of the bonds of the group's collective consciousness and imagination and then developed his own personality. He even added new information about his backstory to the members who had—they thought—dreamed up the fictional accounts about his life.

Applying this to the air museum haunting, theorists suggest that the fictional narrative made people believe there was a ghost. Eventually, consciousness interfaced with reality to produce nearly identical paranormal activity. Skeptics, though, have a quick counter to the tulpa theory. They say that the stories just raised the awareness of staff members and visitors, who then began misattributing natural phenomena. People who are scared tend to see scary things, even though they might just be shadows, or the light reflecting off of surfaces in a strange way. They might hear footsteps when they are actually just normal noises of air traveling through ducts, or the building settling as temperatures shift.

Still, despite the new information about the hoax, reports continue to trickle in. In fact, one of the latest is also one of the most compelling.

The museum's secretary was working one evening and said she heard someone call her name. The voice seemed to emanate from the area where the Avro was parked. She assumed a fellow employee needed her, but when she looked around for the source of the voice, she came to the unsettling discovery that she was alone.

The great thing about museums is that you learn so much with each visit. For instance, that one incident taught the secretary an important lesson: Never walk into the hangar alone. And she never did again.

3

SUPERNATURAL ON THE HIGH SEAS

The Second World War was a hell of a sequel. It was truly global, much more so than World War I. And the war's action did not just happen on the front lines or in the skies above the battlefields, but on the oceans and seas as well. Controlling the world's waterways became key objectives for both Allied and Axis powers. The ferocity of the battles, the number of sailors and airmen, and the amount of boats and ships involved in those battles offer some indication of just how instrumental the oceans were to each side's battle plan.

For the first time, aircraft carriers became key pieces of naval armadas, launching planes to attack land bases and other ships. Battleships remained part of naval power too, prowling the oceans for enemy ships and blasting fortifications prior to sea-based invasions.

And if you're guessing that more conflict creates more casualties and more casualties create more spirit activity, you won't be surprised when you read that something peculiar happened after the war. Many of the vessels that served during the war sailed back to their home countries for a hero's welcome. It would be almost inconceivable to scuttle such heroes or melt them down as scrap, so people raised money to keep them around as museum ships. What they weren't betting on was that not just the physical ships came home; so did the spirits of the men who served on those ships and, in some cases, ghosts of the men they fought. And these floating museums do more than teach visitors about the past; they give them a close-up look at the sailors who fought on the massive warships. Some of those visitors and paranormal investigators, though, say they got too close of a view.

Hundreds of these witnesses—tourists, staff, and invited ghosthunters—say they have encountered things that they couldn't explain while on board these ships, things like weird sounds, strange shadows, and even complete apparitions.

We will have a chance to review their testimonies and more in the pages ahead.

Scares On Board Aircraft Carriers

No weapon formed during World War II received more attention—from friend and foe alike—than American aircraft carriers. They were awe-inspiring in every sense of the term. Every enemy pilot wanted to sink one. Every friendly troop wanted to see one steam his way, because it meant that the extreme punch of these massive warships would soon be brought to bear on the enemy.

After the war, these ships received attention of a different sort. According to paranormal experts, they became targets of supernatural activity.

Three of World War II's most storied flattops, which now serve as museums and learning facilities, are also considered the war's most *ghost-storied* ships. In the next few pages, we'll review the battle history and the supernatural history of the USS *Yorktown*, USS *Hornet*, and USS *Lexington*.

Let's start with the haunted tales and creepy occurrences that have happened aboard the Fighting Lady—the USS *Yorktown*.

The USS *Yorktown:*
A Tourist Attraction Gets Attention
from Paranormal Investigators

She now rests solemnly in Patriots Point, right at the mouth of the calm Cooper River in Charleston Harbor, a boat ride away from Fort Sumter. Visitors can easily spot the aircraft carrier, currently one of a few museum ships on display at Patriots Point, because it completely dominates the harbor. And this lady is special.

Built in an unbelievable sixteen months and change, the USS *Yorktown*, an Essex-class carrier named after the flattop rendered unsalvageable after the Battle of Midway, steamed into battle against the Japanese and never looked back. The sailors, airmen, and Marines aboard battled through World War II—earning eleven battle stars—and then into the Cold War. And, oh yeah, the crew of the *Yorktown* managed to find time to help fish out the astronauts of Apollo 8.

They don't call her the Fighting Lady for nothing.

But is she also the Haunting Lady?

The USS **Yorktown,** *circa 1939.*

Lots of people think so, and not just because scenes from *The Philadelphia Experiment*—a creepy paranormal movie about a possible World War II timeslip incident that we'll discuss later—were filmed on board the *Yorktown*. Dozens of paranormal experts, including the *Yorktown*'s own paranormal historians and some of the world's most famous paranormal investigators have investigated the ship, according to the website Scares and Haunts of Charleston. There are also hundreds of everyday people turned supernatural believers who have their own ghostly encounter stories.

We'll uncover lots of those cases in the pages ahead.

Bruce Orr, a former Charleston detective and accomplished paranormal investigator, is probably the foremost expert on the *Yorktown* hauntings. He's a well-respected guide for ghost tours of the ship and has even written a book about the history and hauntings aboard the USS *Yorktown*. In *Ghosts of the USS* Yorktown: *The Phantoms of Patriots Point*, Orr discusses several of the most intriguing accounts of paranormal experiences on the ship, as well as bits of evidence that suggest that these stories are more than just misidentified natural phenomena or practical jokers telling tall tales.

The number—and the quality—of paranormal encounters seem to rule out the possibility that a sole practical joker is at work, according to experts. It would take a staff of jokers working full-time—especially during the graveyard shift—to pull off pranks equaling the number of supernatural activities that have been reported on the USS *Yorktown*. Some of the phenomena is spectacular. For example, one of the *Yorktown*'s creepiest crewmates is a shadow person—or possibly shadow people—who stalks the ship's dark halls and berths. Witnesses have seen these apparitions so clearly that they mistook them for real people. A Hollywood special effects company would be hard-pressed to create such an illusion. And we should talk about the witnesses, too. The sources of many *Yorktown* haunting stories are not crack-pots by a long shot; they include seasoned veterans, police detectives, and steely-nerved staff members who are rarely thrown by a sudden, but natural creak or crack at night.

Orr had his own weird experiences on board the *Yorktown*. As a veteran investigator and paranormal researcher, Orr typically refrains from labeling every experience he has as paranormal. But you can review Orr's experiences on that night and label it yourself.

The researcher said that he and another associate, who is also interested in the paranormal, had arranged an in-depth investigation of the ship. Specifically, they wanted to investigate the rumors that the ship's hangar deck—the section where old World War II warbirds are currently on display—was haunted. Only two investigators and one or two security personnel would be on board at the time of the investigation. They basically had the ship to themselves.

Or so they thought.

The investigation was barely underway when strange things started to occur. While setting up motion-sensing equipment, they distinctly heard footsteps walk across the catwalk perched directly above them. Orr and his friend stared up, jaws collectively dropping, as the noise passed over them and toward the other end of the ship. They watched as the sound approached the light and saw a shadow blot it out for a second. Orr stayed below while his friend went up the stairs to chase the shadow figure. The friend reported he continued to listen to the footsteps, but could not make contact with the shadow figure.

Both of the security officers were stationed on a floor below them.

That sighting, however, initiated a game of paranormal cat and ghost-mouse for the rest of the investigation. Orr said that after making his rounds, he returned to the hangar deck. As he walked along, he looked up and saw a shadow cut in front of him. The former investigator—like so many other times in his career—wasn't scared off by the strange run-in. It made him curious. And then he would use this curiosity and power of observation to spur on his investigation. Orr remained in place, watching the shadow. A debate raged in his mind, however. Should he just keep watching? Or should he approach the figure?

Orr decided to move toward the shadow—not too fast, not too slow. As he neared the figure, it turned and faded into the darkness. It seemed almost like the shadow sensed Orr was getting too close. Orr located a bench near the museum and sat down to ponder where the motion-sensing equipment should be placed. Strange noises began to issue once again from the section where the investigator last spotted the shadow figures. He went back to the hangar deck and the on-again, off-again chase was back on.

This time, Orr saw not one, but two shadows walk in front of the light and block it momentarily. He now saw the two figures standing near a snack bar. Again, as he began to close in on the shadows, the figures made evasive maneuvers. One faded away and the other stepped back into the shadow.

Orr lists his night on the *Yorktown* as definitely one of his weirder experiences, but does the seasoned investigator believe it was a definite paranormal experience?

"Once again, I am not ready to rubber stamp this experience or the previous one as a 'ghostly' encounter, but what I experienced was not normal and still has me scratching my head wondering what exactly did occur," Orr writes in his book, *Ghosts of the USS Yorktown*.

The investigator might not be ready to classify the behavior on board the *Yorktown* as supernatural, but a long list of witnesses who have encountered the shadow people on the ship might not be as reluctant.

In fact, there are so many shadow people sightings that they've been given a very World War II–flavored nickname. People in the know—staff members and experts on the haunting—who see a shadow person say they've spotted Shadow Ed. Or, more precisely, Shadow E.D., which stands for enemy designated, a World War II expression for coming in contact with an enemy.

And Ed has made himself one of the crew on the *Yorktown*. In fact, he may have been one of the original crew members. According to one story, a security officer at Patriots Point cautiously made his way through the ship on his nightly shift when a sudden feeling—a sixth sense—hit him: "I'm not alone on this shift." The officer turned and saw a "shadowy mass"—and the shadow seemed to be in the shape of a person, not cast by some random object. But no other personnel should have been on board, save the security team—and it wasn't one of his colleagues. The officer quickly contacted the rest of the security team, who assumed an intruder had slipped onto the property. After consulting with them, he considered the sighting real enough to warrant calling in local law enforcement.

It's hard to say what the police officers thought when they arrived on the scene. Maybe some teens came on board as a dare. Maybe the imaginations of security officers who heard one too many tales of Yorky ghosts hit overdrive. Still, officers aren't paid to dismiss possible crimes, they're paid to investigate them. So, they went into action. When the two cops hit the stairwell to the Charleston Naval Shipyard Museum, they both saw something moving a deck below. A large black mass—exactly as described.

Orr writes that the officers later told him they both looked at each other and said, "Did you see that?" at the same time. The investigators quickly turned into paranormal investigators and the hunt was on. As trained observers, they estimated the mass to be about twice the size of a human. The object moved away from them at a fast rate of speed and then ... vanished. Secure doors blocked the exit, so the cops concluded that nothing—at least nothing of the earthly dimension—could have escaped their ever-tightening blockade.

Both officers told Orr they believed the site was secure from human intruders and decided to "let the security team figure it out." Not exactly what the security team, faced with the rest of their shift, wanted to hear.

Galley Ghosts

An army marches on its stomach. Seamen must also sail on their stomachs—and they need a secure line to that food. While soldiers can live off the land, there's no way a sailor can pull into a local restaurant, graze on corn in a farmer's field, or pop into the kitchen of a friendly home on the way to battle.

That makes the galley—or ship's kitchen and mess hall—of a city on the sea like the *Yorktown* so important. It might also be the reason that this area is one of the carrier's most haunted spots.

According to Orr, one *Yorktown* staff member was in charge of cleaning up after a group of high-energy Boy Scouts, who had just finished up their breakfast in the big dining room, during their one-of-a-kind campout on board the grand ship.

The quiet fall morning that descended over the waters became even more silent when the rambunctious scouts receded into other quarters of the ship. The worker—named Lori—was most likely not thinking about ghosts. She had enough on her mind, like a massive cleanup job ahead of her.

The worker wiped down the tables and straightened up the chairs, as she had dozens and dozens of times before. But something was different this time. This morning, things were exceptionally quiet. Weirdly quiet. Pushing the creepy feeling to the back of her mind, she went into the galley, which she started to organize.

That took her about ten minutes, and then she returned to the room she just cleaned. She was not prepared for what awaited. The dining room looked ransacked—the chairs she had pushed neatly under the tables and precisely straightened were now askew. The dining room seemed in worse condition than she found it! Someone, or something, had scattered the chairs, which were now pulled out into the aisle and rested at odd angles.

Any natural explanations she had to explain the incident were weak. If the Boy Scouts came back to wreck the room, they were as silent as ninjas and they only had minutes to work!

Once the worker cleaned up, she did what any other smart person who encountered a blatant example of supernatural activity would do: She ran back to the office and stayed there.

It wasn't the first time a staff member had an encounter with the unknown aboard the *Yorktown* and it would not be the last.

Over the years—and over the many, many reports of the paranormal on board the ship—the guides and workers who spend the most time in the cabins, berths, and decks of the carrier have come to some conclusions about the activity. They don't believe the spirit, or spirits, are trying to harm the staff. They're just playing pranks, probably like the sailors and pilots did to each other to relieve the tensions of war when they sailed on the ship in their corporeal lives.

Once a sailor, always a sailor, they say.

The USS *Hornet:* Raising the Dead

The USS *Hornet*—CV-12—was actually the second carrier named *Hornet* during World War II. The original carrier sunk in the Battle of the Santa Cruz Islands in 1942, and officials rechristened a new Essex class carrier—formerly named USS *Kearsarge—Hornet* in tribute.

Newly christened, the *Hornet* proceeded directly on an aquatic warpath that looked more like a Wild West ride of vengeance for the sinking of her namesake. According to information from the carrier's historic group, the *Hornet* received seven battle stars for her service in the Pacific, including battle stars for the Marianas campaign—also known as the Marianas Turkey Shoot—and Leyte operations.

The USS Hornet, circa 1992.

The battles during World War II and later engagements and missions, including recovering astronauts from sea, did leave some scars. While unscathed by Japanese bombs during the war, many of the *Hornet*'s courageous pilots never made it back to the carrier. Other seamen perished due to illness and accident. The ship, now a tourist attraction and floating museum in Alameda, California, draws the attention of countless people who want to learn more about the ship's history. Other people who visit the *Hornet*, especially the paranormal researchers and those interested in the supernatural, believe that they can actually touch this history by reaching out to the spirits that may still haunt the ship.

Those stories of hauntings come from all walks of life—visitors, former ship hands, staff, historians, etc. And these stories of supernatural encounters can happen at any time—day or night.

Over the past few years, the activity has not necessarily picked up—it would be hard to measure that—but it's definitely become more well-documented. The ship's own website (as well as other blogs and sites) is full of tales from witnesses who have experienced weird activity during their visits. Paranormal researchers have chimed in, too. They tell stories that include a range of unexplainable activity, from the sounds of footsteps walking down—what should be—empty hallways to terrifying shrieks and screams that seem to have no source. People claim to have sensed presences pass by them, or through them, as well as felt temperature spikes. One minute the boat was warm and welcoming, the next it was cold and definitely uninviting. While skeptics easily dismiss claims like these, paranormal investigators have confirmed odd temperature spikes and drops, as well as electromagnetic aberrations.

In the next few pages, we will discuss some of the more vivid encounters documented on the ship.

Dress Whites Ghost

The *Hornet's* most famous spirit has made so many formal appearances on the ship that stories of his visitations have almost become commonplace. A member of a US Coast Guard team volunteering on the *Hornet* said he ran into the ghost while on an errand on the ship.

The guardsman, named Bob, undertook the task of painting a compartment aboard the *Hornet*. He wore a white paper suit to keep clean during the chore. As their paint supply started to run out, Bob decided to fetch some more cans from another coworker. As he walked through the ship, he promptly got lost. He wandered through the narrow passageways, trying to find either his crew or the coworker.

As he navigated around the main passageway on the ship's starboard side—or the right side when you're facing toward the front of the ship—he was startled when a person popped out of the main hall about twenty-five feet from where he stood. Bob figured it was the coworker he was looking for, so he called out to him. But the man kept walking. He watched as the figure walked down the hall and cut into another passageway. Bob followed, but when he got to the hall where he last saw the man, he found that not only was that area chained off, but that the compartment—the only place the man could be—sat completely empty. Not even Houdini could have made that escape.

Baffled, the guardsman managed to rejoin his group of volunteers and later he sought out the coworker he assumed he had stumbled onto during his hunt for paint. Bob asked him why he didn't respond to his call. That was easy, the man said. He wasn't in that area of the ship. In fact, he never left the room where he toiled away for about an hour.

There is no way the figure clad in white walking through the passageway was him, he told Bob. But if it wasn't him and the ship was empty, who did he see? Bob got some answers when he recounted the tale.

One of the *Hornet* employees overheard the conversation and immediately recognized the identity of the mysterious sailor when she heard Bob's description, except it wasn't a living sailor who was making his rounds on the ship. The employee told the workers that the man Bob saw might have been the ghost of one of the *Hornet's* former sailors. She continued, saying that other witnesses who saw the ghost a little more clearly than Bob had noted the figure was decked out in his finest dress whites. The ghost has appeared so often that he earned the nickname "Dress Whites Ghost."

Officer's Ghost and Off-Limits Guests
Another visitor on the ship had a similar run-in with a decorated spirit of the *Hornet* and one that resembles Bob's Dress Whites Ghost.

In an online comment, Kathleen writes that she, her husband, and her aunt toured the *Hornet* a few years ago. Closing time was fast approaching and they neared the end of their tour, so Kathleen's adventurous husband dragged her to a part of the ship that appeared to be off-limits to tourists. The couple wandered through the dimly lit passageways, navigating around piles of surplus equipment.

Kathleen's heart began to beat a little faster and her respiration increased. She felt lost and she had visions of getting arrested for entering an off-limits section of the *Hornet.*

Her worst nightmare then materialized in front of her. She writes that a naval officer in full dress uniform suddenly appeared around the corner.

"I knew for sure we were in trouble," she writes.

But the officer did not bark out orders for the couple to vacate the secure area. He never cast a glance at the scofflaw couple or uttered a word, but just walked right by them. Another weird aspect of the officer struck Kathleen: she never noticed any breeze or wind when he walked closely by her.

Kathleen watched the figure make a crisp turn into one of the rooms. They followed right behind him, except when they got to the room the officer had clearly entered, nobody was in the berth. In fact, like a lot of the other rooms in that section of the ship, bed frames and other pieces of what some might call artifacts and others might call junk filled the berth. There was just no way anyone could maneuver around it. The officer had simply, in her opinion, disappeared.

Although the snappily dressed sailor seemed a bit shy on first sighting, he would make his presence known to the couple in a big way.

Kathleen was beginning to feel unsettled. She started to beg her husband to leave the haunted section of the boat. No sooner had she told him she wanted to leave than her camera ripped away from its strap and crashed to the floor. In the eight years that she'd owned this camera, the strap had never failed, nor has it since.

After her tour, Kathleen had time to reflect on her adventure. She is sure she saw a ghost, and people familiar with the haunted *Hornet* would guess that she saw the Dress Whites Ghost himself.

Fleet Week Meets Freak Week

Fleet Week is a US Navy, Marine Corps, and Coast Guard tradition to dock active military ships recently deployed in overseas operations in a variety of major cities for a week. When thousands of sailors hit the streets of San Francisco during the city's Fleet Week, you're bound to see a lot of weird stuff. But, for one member of the US Naval Sea Cadets, the things he saw—and heard—during Fleet Week in 2005 went beyond weird and will stay with him for the rest of his life.

He writes that he was lucky enough to spend the week on board the USS *Hornet*, a super treat for these cadets, who are young men and women considering enlisting in the US Navy. Even before lights-out, word had spread among the cadets that they were camping on a haunted ship. Unfortunately, at three in the morning, the cadet got called to guard duty, or, as the cadets called it, "fire and security watch." The cadet got dressed and made his way through the cavernous halls of the great ship, joining a few other guards on duty.

Not too long after his watch officially started, his run-ins with the paranormal began, too. Screams echoed down the hall and the cadet sprang into action. He called security and told them that he heard someone scream out in anguish and there must be a medical situation. But when they searched for the source of the screams, no one was there. A few of the guards who also heard the screams joined the security officers looking around the section near where they swore the screams came from, but they couldn't find anything or anyone either. The cries were seemingly coming out of thin air.

An hour later, the spirits returned. This time, it wasn't a sound that jarred the cadet's attention; it was a smell. The cadets caught the scent of a pipe or cigar and immediately called for security. They figured someone must have slipped out of the bunk for a smoke. Security, however, said they saw a smoker in the fantail section of the ship. They tried to find him.

As they searched, the security detail heard footsteps thumping across the deck above them. They rushed to investigate, but just like with the phantom screamer, as soon as they reached the section, it was empty and silent.

The writer admits he was already a believer in the supernatural. However, after spending a night aboard the *Hornet*, the cadet said his beliefs in the supernatural have deepened.

"It had to be the scariest thing I have ever done," he writes.

He's not the only one who has been spiritually affected by his visit on the *Hornet*. Loyd Auerbach, one of the world's most respected parapsychologists, said that based on reports from volunteers, staff, and visitors there could be as many as fifty ghosts on the ship. He tells several stories of his own encounters with the ship's ghosts in interviews and especially on his YouTube channel, which you can find in the notes section of this book.

The USS *Lexington*:
True Ghost Encounters Aboard the Blue Ghost

The Japanese sailors and airmen who fought in the Pacific were afraid of a ghost. They called it the Blue Ghost. Like a vengeful spirit, this ghost appeared out of nowhere and would suddenly unleash unholy hell on the Japanese forces. We know the Blue Ghost as the USS *Lexington*.

But there's another reason for its supernatural nickname.

The USS Lexington, *circa 2014.*

In 1942, news quickly circulated among the Japanese that the *Lexington*—that monster of the seas—had finally been sunk during the Battle of the Coral Sea.

Imagine their horror, then, when just a few months later, they saw the USS *Lexington* steaming toward them. They had no way of knowing that the superpowered American war machine had produced the new USS *Lexington* (CV-16) almost as soon as the old USS *Lexington* (CV-2) had settled to the floor of the Coral Sea. The Japanese forces were stunned. And scared. Throughout the war, the Japanese read reports and heard rumors that the new *Lexington* had been sunk no less than four times. Yet, right after they read the reports, there she sailed, turning into the wind and catapulting her planes skyward to bomb their ships, down their aircraft, and strafe their gun positions.

But the Blue Ghost is not done haunting, according to some.

Although the USS *Lexington*, like a lot of her fellow "scarecraft carriers," is no longer at war, she's not at peace either. There is a constant stream of reports from her new base in Corpus Christi, Texas, where she serves as a museum ship, that spirits continue to stalk the decks and berths of the big boat.

The Ghost of Charlie

The haunting of the *Lexington* is spread out over a few locations, but perhaps the most haunted spot is the engine room. Ship historians say that the rabid Japanese military staged numerous attacks to sink the Blue Ghost that haunted them so much. Those attacks led to many casualties. At least one of those casualties—a man who worked in the engine room—continues to keep watch on his beloved ship.

Visitors have said that they sense a peculiar presence when they enter the engine room. While it's hard to describe, they say they feel like someone is watching them. Other visitors have seen a more visible display of some unknown force. They say they have watched doors and hatches open on their own with nobody nearby, and no external force— like a breeze—evident.

Because the ship is open to the public and the rumors of hauntings have circulated extensively, lots of paranormal research groups, amateur ghosthunters, and people just looking for a good scare have treated the *Lexington* like a supernatural laboratory. Some of their stories are startling.

One visitor initially felt normal when he and members of his family arrived on the ship to take in a historic adventure. Once he started to descend into the ship, however, he had a sensation that another visitor—an unseen visitor—was taking the tour with him. As the man snapped pictures, he became aware of unsettling temperature shifts, too. First the room boiled, then it turned cold. As they probed deeper into the ship's lower decks, the presence became physical. He felt something brush against his legs.

The man and his cousin entered the hospital wing, still equipped with some of the medical instruments of the time. The visitor's cousin started to crack jokes about a ghost shooting him with one of the needles on display, which isn't always the wisest thing to say in a paranormally intense environment. Soon, the cousin began to experience actual pinches and pokes. Marks began to appear on the cousin's body, ones that weren't there just a few minutes before.

Fortunately, the tour was almost over and the family of would-be ghosthunters exited without further incident.

Other visitors have encountered spirits in the ship's engine room, although these run-ins seem more benign than the spectral doctor giving out supernatural shots in the hospital wing. People seem to think the ghost there is a friendly one. They say they feel something pass by them as they enter the room, others feel a cool chill. A few witnesses watch in shock as doors slowly close. And again it doesn't seem to be an errant breeze shutting the door, there seems to be a definite force purposely pushing the door closed.

Then there are the Charlie sightings, according to writer Eric Mills, who discusses some of the hauntings on board the *Lexington* in his book *The Spectral Tide: True Ghost Stories of the U.S. Navy.*

Most experts on the hauntings suggest that the disembodied presence that is detected in the engine room may be related to claims from witnesses who have actually seen a shape—if not an actual apparition—in the engine room or near it. Sometimes the shape is just that—a shadow or a blurry image staring thoughtfully at the equipment in the engine room. Others see something far more terrifying—a full-bodied apparition.

A few people offer the rarest type of ghostly run-in with the Blue Ghost's ghost—they say the spirit served as their tour guide. According to the reports, the guests boarded the ship to take a self-guided tour around the *Lexington*. As luck would have it, just as they boarded, a blonde-haired, blue-eyed sailor offered to lead them on a personal tour. He must be some type of reenactor, they thought. He was wearing an incredibly accurate World War II naval uniform. "Maybe he's a paid tour guide or a volunteer," they speculated. The guide really knew what he was talking about, too. "It's like he actually served on the *Lexington* in World War II," they thought.

In this instance, the guide said his name was Charlie and urged them to follow him. His knowledge of the ship was phenomenal, the group agreed. He recounted stories from the war and reminisced about some of his old shipmates. "What a performance," the tourists thought. "This guy should be an actor."

Then, Charlie guided them deeper into the ship's massive interior and the tour continued. However, the guests said that the tour guide suddenly became distracted and broke away from them. He walked faster and faster. Some of the guests tried to keep up, some—too busy checking out all the displays and fascinated by all the equipment—never noticed that the guide had left the group.

According to the report, Charlie rounded the corner and disappeared off of the face of the earth. Despite a search, the tourists—stranded in the inner recesses of the massive World War II warship—could not find their guide.

Once the guests got their bearings and made it back to the surface of the ship, they searched for other staff members, perhaps to complain about the abruptly ended tour. When they chatted with staff and described their tour guide, the staff member's reply terrified the guests. The guide—a living and breathing one this time—told them that, based on the visitor's description of a blonde, blue-eyed man dressed in World War II uniform, no such employee fitting that likeness existed. To the staff's knowledge, no reenactor was on the ship at that time either.

So, who is Charlie? There is a lot of speculation among the ghost-loving paranormal enthusiasts who use the ship as a hunting ground for supernatural activity. Of course, the names Charles, Charly, and Charlie crop up on the *Lexington*'s personnel ledgers and documents. It's a common name. However, some believe that Charlie is the ghost of one of the sailors who died on board, while others believe it is the ghost of someone who served on the ship—and just really loved the experience. He keeps returning now to show off his prized Blue Ghost to people who visit the floating museum.

If these reports came from a bunch of tourists who claim to see apparitions on board the ship, that would be one thing. But paranormal experts who have investigated the case say that many staff members—some of them former skeptics—report run-ins with Charlie, along with other spirits. They also say they've collected impressive evidence from the ship's ghost cameras and through the collection of EVPs.

One of the former skeptics is tour guide David Deal. He is not only an expert about the *Lexington*, but a former sailor who served on the ship. He eventually rose through the ranks and became a catapult chief for carrier operations. His skepticism started to falter when he heard a story from a visitor who told him some tour guide offered a lesson about the engine room equipment. When Deal quizzed the visitor on the tour guide's lessons, the man gave answers so detailed that Deal doubted a common person could have made it up. Then the tourist began to offer other bits of information. It was stuff that even Deal, an expert who served on the *Lexington*, did not know. This information, Deal came to believe, obviously came from someone who served on the Lex during World War II. And no tour guide on the staff fit the description offered by the tourist. Deal became convinced it was no tour guide who spoke with these visitors—it was one of the *Lexington*'s helpful spirits.

Another high-ranking staff member of the museum had his own encounter with spirits and possibly with Charlie. A director of operations and exhibits said that on several separate occasions, he has stepped from his office and caught the distinct sound of clothes rustling and footsteps. He expects to see a coworker or guest, but a quick scan of the area reveals he is all alone.

Charlie doesn't just give tours, according to one crew member. He lends a helping hand. Members of a paint crew said they knocked off for lunch one day. They were about halfway done with the project. When they came back about an hour or so later, the rest of the room was painted. The team credited Charlie with the work.

Tales seem to indicate that apparently Charlie has many ghostly comrades on the Blue Ghost. And former enemies are now welcome too, it seems. One couple said they saw a dark-haired man dressed in work clothes—a description that doesn't sound like the fair-haired Charlie, *Lexington* haunting experts point out—jump from one deck to the one below. When they rushed to the lower deck, expecting to find an injured man, there was no one there. Others have claimed to see a man dressed as an American sailor and a man who looks like a Japanese aviator standing together at the end of the hall. As they approach the two men, they disappear.

Reenactors? A case of mistaken identity? Or could it be that the *Lexington* has become the haunted meeting place for both former allies and former enemies?

The Blue Ghost and the other haunted carriers have converted skeptics. People have changed their minds about the supernatural after witnessing some of the strange activity aboard the *Lexington*. But many skeptics remain. Weird but totally natural explanations, misidentified phenomena, and the plain old failure of human perceptive systems get most of the blame from skeptics. The back-and-forth between skeptics and believers has turned into evidence gathering. The staff has placed security cameras at various locations on the *Lexington*, which are now serving as handy ghost cameras. They also invited some famous ghosthunting crews on tours.

The search, as they say, goes on.

Putting the Dread in Dreadnaughts—
Haunted Battleships and Other Warships

There was a little bit of rivalry between crews of aircraft carriers and battleships. The big dreadnaughts, after all, were the undisputed stars of the naval arsenal for decades, if not centuries. The battleship lineage goes back to *ship of the line* sailing ships that packed a dozen-plus guns belowdecks and carried the power of a country's might across oceans.

Ironclad ships appeared in the American Civil War and only became more powerful and more deadly.

But the upstart aircraft carrier threatened the battleship's supremacy.

In the next pages we'll see that a new rivalry exists: which type of ship—the battleship or the aircraft carrier—packs the biggest paranormal punch? We'll let you decide.

The USS *North Carolina:*
Showboat Ghosts

While the aircraft carriers earned their share of press and glory, the battleship served as the workhorse of World War II, from the beginning to the end of the conflict. The German battleship *Schleswig-Holstein* probably fired the first shots of World War II when its crew unleashed a withering bombardment on Polish troops stationed in Westerplatte. The Japanese surrender officially occurred on board the battleship USS *Missouri*.

The USS North Carolina, anchored in Cape Fear, near Wilmington, North Carolina.

Battleships were ruthless warriors in hundreds of engagements at sea during the war, the targets of hundreds of attacks, and the scenes of an incalculable number of acts of courage and valor. If you think these old battlewagons could tell some stories, you would be right.

And some of those are ghost stories.

One ship that has earned a reputation on both fronts—haunted and hallowed—is the USS *North Carolina*, also called the "Showboat." It was involved in just about every major naval engagement in the Pacific during World War II.

Apparitions of sailors lost during battles have appeared to several witnesses who served on the ship during the war and after the conflict, while other witnesses say they have observed and experienced a range of paranormal phenomena that have convinced them that the big ship is haunted. In fact, the hauntings and hints of hauntings have become so numerous that paranormal investigators—including some of the biggest names in the field—have joined in the hunt for proof of ghosts aboard the *North Carolina*. We will explore those accounts and legends now.

Ghostly Smile

One group that has conducted the most thorough investigations of these haunting goings-on aboard the USS *North Carolina* and documented those adventures is Port City Paranormal. They probed the big boat back in 2009 and came back with an honest assessment that included some debunking. However, they also collected evidence that seems to back up many of the witnesses who claimed to experience haunted activity aboard the ship.

A Port City Paranormal member, Jane Anderson, said the paranormal research group was established in 2004. With education and training from the Rhine Research Center, the team has taken part in an in-depth chronicling of the spirit activity on the USS *North Carolina*—gathering information and evidence, as well as theorizing why spirits are haunting the ship.

"There is much more to investigating than stalking spirits in the dark," Jane told me. "Our main goal is to explore the human experience and life after death. We believe that what you were in life is what you are in death. In other words, the personality survives."

According to Jane, her most memorable encounter during the team's extensive study of the ship occurred as she walked down the completely dark passageway on the third deck. As she made her way down the hall, she noticed a small point of light. She had no idea what the source of the light could possibly be.

The light drew closer and closer until it stood right in front of her—and that's when Jane realized it wasn't really a light at all. She was staring right into a pair of blue eyes and saw the gleam of a wide smile.

"The smile was unmistakable," Jane said. "It was difficult to describe, but the hair seemed to just float around his head and the hair had a reddish tinge to it."

Other apparitions made themselves known—often in dramatic fashion.

One night, after everyone else had gone home, Jane and her husband, Doug, found themselves alone on the ship. They continued their exploration, going deeper into the ship and eventually pausing in engine room number three. That's when a strange feeling hit Jane.

"I felt as if someone was standing next to my right shoulder," said Jane. "I was afraid to look, so I asked Doug to look."

He turned and saw a tall, blonde man standing right beside Jane—right where she felt the presence. As Doug and the spirit made eye contact, the ghost smiled and began to fade away. While Jane had spent a considerable amount of time in the archives as a volunteer, Doug never visited the archives and wasn't familiar with the pictures of the sailors who served—and died—on the ship. Jane decided to run a test on her husband's ghost sighting.

She copied photos of a random group of men who served on the USS *North Carolina*, including a man who was killed during the deadly Japanese attack. She then spread them out on their dining room table. She asked her husband to look at each picture and pick the one who looked like the apparition he witnessed.

Doug did not hesitate. He immediately pointed to one picture. Jane knew right away that this was a photo of one of the sailors killed during the torpedo attack on the USS *North Carolina*.

Over the years, the couple and their team amassed more evidence—including videos and EVPs—most of which is documented and archived on the group's website. They also volunteered to help with the restoration. Jane became a docent—a volunteer guide or teacher—and also spent considerable time researching the daily lives of the men who served and fought on the ship. That research gave Jane additional insights into some of the paranormal activity that they—and dozens of other witnesses—encountered on the ship.

Most paranormal theorists would point to the USS *North Carolina*'s dead as the prime suspects behind the haunting. Perhaps these spirits do linger, suggested Jane, but spirits of those killed during their service on the ship might not explain all of the activity. Some of the paranormal activity might be related to the emotional energy left-over from the ship's warriors.

"The main energy that fuels the activity is that of the many young men who served on the USS *North Carolina*," Jane said. "The boys of the battleship were energetic and devoted to the fight for our country and our freedom. To many of the young men that fought this may have been the most exciting time of their lives."

The Night Watchman's Spooky Perspective

There are a lot of things not to like about being a night security officer on the USS *North Carolina*.

It's dark. It's lonely. And it can be, well, kind of creepy.

But, for someone who doesn't mind the paranormal, or even invites it into their lives, it's the best job ever.

Maybe Danny Bradshaw likes the paranormal or maybe he doesn't, but he's seen plenty of it on board the USS *North Carolina* while working as a night watchman. It's not like he wasn't warned. Even before he got the job, Bradshaw, who wrote the book *Ghosts on the Battleship North Carolina* about his experiences, received warnings. He said the man who held the position before him, a friend of his, told him that he should expect to see things on the ship that might test his assumptions about the world around us and the unseen world that lies beneath or above us.

Bradshaw remembers his first encounter with that unseen world. He said it was pitch black that night—of course, as a night watchman, it was always dark on the ship—but there was something else going on. He had a weird feeling. Well, it could have been a feeling, or it could have been a premonition. This strange sensation grew as he walked toward a power box in the ship's galley, a single beam of light emanating from his flashlight and crisscrossing the pathway in front of him. Adding to the creepy effect, the section that Bradshaw walked through was filled with faceless cardboard silhouettes of sailors, to give visitors a better visual idea of how the men lived aboard the USS *North Carolina* when she was in action. The cutouts may have been helpful for tourists, but at night when you are all alone, they look pretty freaky, Bradshaw admits. In any event, Bradshaw finally reached the power box without incident. But as soon as he did, a sudden, cold breeze hit him and a hand gripped him firmly on his shoulder.

Footsteps echoed across the room. He swung his flashlight beam toward the sound and caught—for an instant—a sailor just standing in an open hatch! It was definitely not one of the cardboard cutouts. In fact, the flashlight's beam cut right through the sailor, like he was transparent. Bradshaw said the spirit appeared so alive that he could make out features, such as his blonde—almost white—hair. The sight scared Bradshaw so much that he let out a scream. With that, the spirit of the sailor disappeared and Bradshaw began shaking. He turned and ran out of the room, but he soon learned that although he could run, he couldn't hide from the supernatural forces at work on the ship.

As he descended the ladder to escape the clutches of the spirit sailor, he stopped long enough to hear footsteps coming down the ladder above him. He couldn't go back up! He continued down the ladder and ran toward the other side of the ship for his alternative escape route. As Bradshaw ran, he prayed, "Please, God, let me out. I don't want to die here."

The prayer worked. Bradshaw was somehow able to run to safety.

Bradshaw, like many witnesses of the ship's paranormal power, wonders what is behind the haunting. The battleship has been the scene of plenty of violent incidents and even deaths. Historians tell us that about ten people have died on board the ship—a few from direct action during World War II, a few from mishaps and friendly fire. For paranormal researchers, this is a no-brainer. Places where dramatic scenes of violence and death have played out tend to be places where you will find ghosts and other paranormal activity. Boats are no exception. That may explain some of the ghosts, according to Bradshaw.

Over the years of paranormal run-ins—or, in some cases, the paranormal run-outs—Bradshaw has developed some of his own theories about the spirit that haunts the ship. In fact, he says there are spirits, plural, that haunt the *North Carolina*. There are some good spirits and possibly at least one not so good, if not evil, spirit behind the activity.

The good ones primarily just engage in aggravating activities, possibly as a way to reach out to Bradshaw and let him know they're around. The spirits turn lights off and slam doors, along with moving items in the room around.

But Bradshaw knows when the evil spirit is present. He says the temperature drops so much that he can see his own breath, even in summer, in the bowels of the super humid ship. Bradshaw says this ghost screams at him, and he's felt so threatened by the entity that he's run from it. But the ghost chases him. These encounters with the evil entity can last a few minutes.

He told Alison Parker, a reporter from *News & Record*, "Two things bother me: He can physically move things, and there's evil in 'im … I don't know if he's saving something up for me. It makes me wonder if there's going to be a night he's going to do something bad."

You wouldn't be the first to suggest that maybe all of these apparitions and phantom arguments are just part of Bradshaw's overactive imagination, but one unsettling fact intrudes: Bradshaw's friends have seen them too, and so have visitors on the ship. These ghosts didn't just hide around and wait for night. They appeared in broad daylight, sometimes as public tours were rolling through the ship, Bradshaw says.

Another group—Bedford Paranormal—may have uncovered some evidence of the haunting's source, as well. Some of the supernatural manifestations may relate to the torpedo attack on the ship during World War II. According to historians, four men died when a Japanese torpedo found its mark near the area where the ship's latrine is located. Four men were in the latrine when the explosion—and ensuing rush of water—ripped into the space.

Emergency protocol insisted that the doors to the area must be shut so that the water did not flood the undamaged areas. The sailors quickly sealed off the latrine area. The area remained sealed, even though they could hear the screams of a man who survived the attack, but was stuck in the latrine as it rapidly filled with water. He banged desperately on the door. Still, the sailors did their duty. They knew more water would take more lives, perhaps jeopardizing the whole ship. This heartbreaking decision, according to later reports, deeply affected the rest of the sailors.

When the team from Bedford Paranormal explored the ship during a tour led by Bradshaw, one member of the group noticed some odd behavior from a nearby berth. The light would dim suddenly and then regain its full glare.

The phenomena—like someone had walked in front of the light in that room—happened over and over again. Another ghosthunter on the tour saw the light show too, and he went to investigate. Once the ghosthunter entered the room, the light steadied. As soon as the investigator returned to the group, the light began to flicker again. One theory is that the spirit of the sailor who became trapped in the ship during the attack is still in the room and he was hiding from the living human presence.

The Port City Paranormal team also gathered some evidence—the hard way—that confirmed Bradshaw's suspicion that either, at best, a spirit with a prankster sense of humor or, at worst, a malicious entity, remained on the battleship. First, the team's spirit-sensing equipment was tripped—a better description is that the device went berserk—and then a few members claimed something harassed them during their investigation. In particular, blonde females with the group reported that something tugged at their hair.

At least one of the investigators went beyond being convinced that the USS *North Carolina* was haunted—she won't return to the ship.

It's interesting to note that other female investigators report they have also received this unwanted attention. Researcher Jane Anderson, for instance, said she may have even been the recipient of a ghost goose at one point during an investigation. If you think sailors are bad when they hit port after being away at sea for a few months, imagine what they're like when they are locked on a ship for eternity.

Beyond the anecdotal evidence, the team said they listened to one clip and it sounded like big guns booming. The noise resembled the newsreel footage of the Showboat in action during the war.

This team, along with dozens of other paranormal investigators and hundreds of employees and visitors, believe that the battleship is haunted. Time, they say, just cannot silence the indomitable spirit of the USS *North Carolina* or her crew.

The USS *Arizona:*
Solemn Spirits of the USS *Arizona* Memorial

It was a cold, calculated act that brought a reluctant America into World War II, guns blazing. The Japanese attack on Pearl Harbor, meant to stun the country quickly into submission, did the opposite: it incurred the wrath of a nation that was previously safe and content to remain in the relative isolation that her two oceans offered.

December 7, 1941, a date that lives in infamy, also lives on in unexpected, unexplained ways, according to paranormal theorists and hundreds of witnesses. People believe that Pearl Harbor is now haunted by spirits whipped up by the same flames of passion, patriotism, fear, and anger that ignited the country into action decades ago.

The USS Arizona, circa January 1941.

Although most of the sailors, airmen, Marines, and soldiers who served at Pearl are now gone, more than their memory is alive today at the Hawaiian base. Some say the psychological intensity of the battle may have etched itself in the spirits and the souls of those who lost their lives in the attack. And they return, even after all these years.

It comes as no surprise to the experts of the paranormal that the USS *Arizona* Memorial—the solemn center of remembrance at Pearl Harbor—is also a hub for supernatural phenomena at the base. The memorial is built over the top of the wreckage of the battleship, which took the brunt of the horrendous Japanese bombing run on the base. That type of emotional intensity and that level of tragedy tends to naturally attract anomalous activity, paranormal theorists suggest.

These experts and believers in the paranormal have no trouble believing that ghosts stalk the *Arizona*. It is more than a memorial. After all, it's actually the tomb for more than a thousand sailors and officers who served on the battleship, one of the jewels of America's Pacific fleet, on that early December morning when a flurry of bombs hit the ship. One of the bombs crashed into ammunition magazines, detonating a catastrophic explosion.

As a tourist attraction, the memorial is the subject of thousands—hundreds of thousands—of pictures. In addition to the photogenic quality of the Hawaiian base, visitors just want to take home a long-term memento of their journey to the site. But some tourists say they got more than that—they believe they have evidence of an eternal reminder. In some of the shots, weird shapes and oddly lit orbs of light are visible, ones that the photographers swear weren't in the frame when they snapped it. Over the years, people visiting the *Arizona* have taken photos that show orbs, oddly shaped shadows, and even what appear to be images of people. These images are often foggy, or appear as human-shaped mist, according to some reports. EVPs popping up on digital cameras and smartphone screens are one thing, but actually seeing a ghost is another.

One of the ghost tales told most often is the story about a sailor tasked with morning watch right before the attack. The story says that the man briefly left his post on the deck of the *Arizona*. Minutes later, the Japanese planes zoomed in and dropped their lethal cargo. The sailor and hundreds of other men were killed instantly.

The figure of a sailor is said to appear near where the USS *Arizona* once docked, usually on misty mornings during low tide. He is seen—on eternal watch now—looking out onto the memorial. Some speculate that he is perhaps driven by remorse or guilt for leaving his watch at the worst possible time.

It's not just electronic phenomena and misty apparitions that point toward a supernatural occupation of the naval base. Some say you can hear the ghosts of the past. Alarm bells blare near the memorial. Often, the alarms sound like they are ringing in an unknown spot in the distance. Other visitors have reported that the sound is so clear, so loud, and so persistent that they believe the alarm bells are part of some ghostly reenactment or service. But, of course, no alarm bells are part of the memorial.

Photographic Evidence that Even the Harbor Is Haunted

Another hotly debated piece of Pearl Harbor paranormal is whether ghostly images of the sailors who died in the attack can be seen in the waves that undulate throughout the base's pristine waters. No one—to my knowledge—has ever distributed a picture of the mournful misty ghost who failed on his watch, but a photo was taken of a water ghost and has made its way around the internet.

According to one report on the website Mysterious Universe, an Australian tourist named Susan De Vanny was visiting Pearl Harbor on September 26, 2011. As Susan and her family toured the base, she—like the hundreds of other visitors there—was taking pictures just about as fast as her finger could tap the button of her digital camera.

At a certain point, De Vanny decided she had enough photos. In fact, she might have too many, so she wanted to delete the unneeded shots. Taking a pause in her tour, she sat down and clicked through the digital pictures, carefully eyeing them to see if she should keep them or not. Some photos instantly did not make the cut. The lighting wasn't right, or the picture was blurry and out of focus. Noticing some distortion on one photo, she put her finger on the delete button when she noticed something peculiar about the photo that filled the camera's screen. Something strange appeared in the water.

As De Vanny inspected a blurry section of the photograph more closely, she suddenly saw the unmistakable image of a man—a young man—staring back at her. Without pointing out what she saw, De Vanny enlisted a few other family members to examine the photograph on their own. She didn't point out the shape that she saw in the water, but her husband saw it instantly—it was a face.

The revelation gave De Vanny and her family a moment to pause and reflect on the great sacrifice of these young men.

She said, "It just looked really sad, really sad and young … I don't know if it represents the men at that time who perished."

Not all the skeptics are convinced by the photographic evidence. They say that people are pattern seekers. We look at random elements of nature, such as a cloud, and see objects or people—for example, Mickey Mouse, a horse, the ghost of a long dead hero, and so on. These skeptics say the face in the oil-slicked water is nothing more than that.

Fortunately, there are places on the web you can find the photo and judge for yourself. A link—or links—is provided in this book's notes and bibliography section.

Despite the photographic evidence and the tons of other spooky stories from Pearl Harbor—for instance, in the section on haunted airplanes and air bases, you can read about some of the supernatural happenings on Hickam Air Base near Pearl Harbor—it's important to note also that some of the biggest skeptics include the park service who looks after the site. Officially, they say there are no ghosts.

The USS *The Sullivans* (DD-537): A Haunting Family Legacy

The mission of the old naval battle wagons of World War II isn't over quite yet. After years of staring down the barrels of the most impressively armed and best-trained navies that the United States ever faced, several of the ships in the Pacific fleet have been reassigned to serve as classrooms and as eternal monuments to the brave sailors who once worked and fought on those vessels.

That's probably why one couple decided to pay a visit to the museum ships that are open to the public in the Buffalo Naval Park. They wanted to take in some history up close and personal. They had no idea how close.

Not too long into their visit, they realized they made a mistake. It was off-season and the exhibits were closed. But luck suddenly turned in their favor. An officer—he looked like an admiral—was on board the Fletcher-class destroyer, the USS *The Sullivans*. The ship is a veteran of some of the Pacific's bloodiest battles and now rests in the relatively calm waters of Lake Erie, of all places.

Not only did the admiral let the couple aboard the ship, but he gave them a personal tour. However, something weird and different struck them about their highly decorated guide. He was a little distant at times. And some of the stories he told contained highly detailed information and could be a little graphic, like the one he told in the fire room about the sailor who was burned in an accident there.

Of course, after their tour was over, they couldn't help but brag about it. But, when they bragged about the tour, they found some disconcerting information from people who questioned their account. They found out, for instance, that there was no admiral at the park—then, or ever. Not only that, but the guides don't dress up in uniforms, and certainly not the uniform of an admiral.

With a shudder, the couple realized they may have just been the latest victims of the USS *The Sullivans* haunting.

A Band of Five Brothers

The haunting of the USS *The Sullivans* allegedly began on another ship decades ago and thousands of miles away on the waves of the war-torn Pacific Ocean.

Five brothers from Iowa, the Sullivan boys—Albert, 20; Madison, 23; Joseph, 24; Francis, 26, and George, 27—were serving aboard the USS *Juneau* in 1942.

The boys had agreed to join the Navy as long as they served together. Nothing would separate this close-knit family. Nothing.

On November 13, 1942, as the destroyer took part in the Battle of the Guadalcanal campaign, a lurking Japanese submarine would send a torpedo crashing into the thin armor of the Juneau and test that brotherly bond. The torpedo, according to reports, landed close to the ammunition magazine. A huge explosion nearly ripped the ship apart. The *Juneau*—or what was left of it—quickly sank.

The captain of a nearby ship, which could have rescued survivors, did not chance a rescue effort. He doubted that anyone survived the conflagration and worried that the sub might target the rest of the task force. A call to send a rescue craft to the scene was not transferred until much later because a rule requiring radio silence was in effect.

Unbelievably, about one hundred of the seven hundred-man crew survived the explosion and found themselves stranded in the ocean. Reportedly, two of the Sullivan brothers—Al and George—were among the survivors. Al, however, drowned shortly after the sinking. According to a small group of survivors, the grief caused by the loss of his brothers then drove George to such despair that he jumped off of the relative safety of a life raft in a desperate attempt to find and rescue his brothers.

On January 12, 1943, back in Iowa, Thomas, the father of the Sullivan boys, was just about to leave his home for work when three men in uniform—a doctor, a lieutenant commander, and a chief petty officer—appeared on his porch.

One of the officers spoke up. "I have some news for you about your boys," he said.

"Which one?" Thomas asked.

"I'm sorry," he replied. "All five."

The loss of all five sons at once did more than devastate the husband and wife; it changed history. Officials changed military policy so that surviving family members could avoid serving in combat or being drafted if the family already lost members in the war. The plot of the movie *Saving Private Ryan* revolves around this idea.

In a magnanimous tribute to the American heroes, the Navy named a new destroyer bound for the Pacific after the brothers. The tribute, however, may have not just invoked the name of the fighting Sullivan family, but it may have invoked their spirits as well. As evidence, some of the crew members who served on the USS *The Sullivans* point to the relative luck the ship had during the war, avoiding any major damage or loss of life. These sailors point to the Sullivan boys as spirit-bound protectors of the ship.

Paranormal theorists claim other stories prove the brothers are now in eternal service aboard their namesake vessel. Since the dedication of the ship, sailors on board the USS *The Sullivans* also reported experiencing strange activity that they believed was tied to one, if not all, of the brothers. One of the first documented supernatural reports circulated soon after the ship was retired in 1969. According to one account, workers saw a heavy wrench levitate off a table and sail across the room.

Today, the ship serves as a living museum of what life was like on a World War II destroyer. As incidents that appear to defy rational explanations—incidents similar to the case of the flying wrench—continue to occur, the floating museum and tribute to the Sullivans may also give staff and visitors a lesson about what the afterlife may be like.

One longtime staff member reported he's had more than a few personal lessons over the years.

The Graveyard Shift

Eddie Kirkwood, a staff member who worked a lot of night shifts on the USS *The Sullivans*, has reported several of those weird occurrences—ones that, for him, defy rational explanations, according to *The Generation*, a student newspaper for the University of Buffalo.

One night, Kirkwood was asked to paint a fresh set of yellow lines on the floor of the ship. He placed the yellow paint on a table and prepared to work. Before he could, though, he watched as the paint can sailed off the table and smashed on the wall. The paint went everywhere. Then, as the paranormal fury reached a crescendo, a welding shield began to swirl around a fire extinguisher.

Kirkwood tried desperately to explain away the activity. Maybe the wind blew the shield? But it's doubtful a breeze could be generated in the deep center of the ship. The door was shut. All the fans or vacuums had been turned off, too.

The worker did what a lot of us would do if they experienced something this out of the ordinary—he went home. Well, he actually ran home.

Whatever was trying to get Kirkwood's attention did so in a quick hurry. And it wouldn't be the last time the spirits of the USS *The Sullivans* would be in contact with the man.

Kirkwood knew he wasn't the only worker with the unenviable job of watching over the haunted ship at night. He had heard plenty of stories about the ship—and actually the park itself, because other sites in the area were also rumored to be haunted. But the ghost stories about the USS *The Sullivans* had generally made the rounds throughout the community of World War II history buffs that visited Buffalo Naval Park, as well as groups of paranormal investigators. In 1989, a worker traveled below deck and got the shock of his life. He saw the floating torso and head of a man coming toward him. The face was bloody and burnt.

He wouldn't be the only worker pestered not by a bad boss or dreadful duties on the job, but by the ship's restless spirits. For example, another man who worked as a night watchman before Kirkwood heard a voice yell, "Hey you!" Other employees say the ghosts on the USS *The Sullivans*, who many presume are one—or all—of the Sullivans, can get physical. One worker woke up on the hard deck of the ship. It's certainly not a place to sneak a nap during his shift. He had no idea how he got there and believes some mysterious and invisible force knocked him unconscious.

Kirkwood's next experience in the haunted naval park rattled him even more. The USS *Little Rock*, which is another ship in the harbor, often plays host to parties and receptions. Kirkwood worked a party on that ship one night. As he mixed with the party attendees, they began to thank him for putting on a little bit of an extra show for them. Kirkwood was confused. He had no idea what they were talking about, but he played along. They then pointed to a spinning radar dish.

It made for a pretty cool party effect, they all agreed.

Kirkwood, however, didn't consider this the naval version of a spinning disco ball entertainment at all. He knew that he had turned off the circuit breaker that killed the power to the radar. There was no reason for it to be activated. Allowing the guests to believe he turned on the radar for their benefit, the employee never let on that something was amiss, but he did file the incident away on a long list of the very weird activities that he witnessed on this ship and on the USS *The Sullivans*, as well as other places in the haunted Buffalo Naval Park.

Although staff members seem to have the most exposure to the ghosts of the USS *The Sullivans*, casual visitors have also amassed a miscellaneous list of strange experiences, including the feeling of a presence that follows them through their tour, hearing the sound of someone whispering in their ears, and watching hatches open by themselves.

Researching the USS **The Sullivans**

All these reports of strange happenings have attracted another type of visitor to the park, except these visitors are on a mission—they want to either prove or debunk paranormal activity once and for all. One of the members of the staff, John Branning, is a former naval engineer who told a reporter that he considers himself a skeptic, but admits that the number of strange incidents makes it hard to discount. He mentioned the dozens of paranormal research groups that recorded voices and noises as they collected their EVPs. They also find shapes and orbs in the pictures they snap. The engineer has also witnessed sensitives—people who can detect spiritual presences—become overwhelmed on *The Sullivans*.

He said that anomalous mechanical failures have become routine. Batteries—fully charged on shore—become drained and lifeless once they are carried on board. Many paranormal researchers believe this is a sign that an entity is using the power from the battery to manifest in the world.

Skeptics answer that these experiences are easy to explain; people who expect to find evidence of ghosts find evidence of ghosts. Though their experiences may not be evidence, those who served—and continue to serve—on the USS *The Sullivans,* and the history buffs who tour the ship, remain convinced that the spirits of five brothers united during life have remained united during death to serve the ship they once guarded and the country they loved.

4

WORLD WAR II'S GHOSTLY LEADERS

Douglas MacArthur once claimed that "old soldiers never die, they simply fade away." He apparently didn't know some of his comrades and enemies very well. The spirits of these World War II warriors never truly faded away.

Numerous ghost stories about famous World War II generals and political leaders fill the pages of Weird War II history. They also span the continents that were involved in those conflicts. Some of the names—and especially the places that they haunt—may surprise you.

We'll start our examination of those ghostly generals, phantom field marshals, and at least one paranormal prime minister now, with one of the war's most tenacious fighters. He was so tenacious that family members say he fought a rearguard action against death so he could deliver one last message to his loved ones.

Old Blood and Ghosts:
General George S. Patton

"Old Blood and Guts." General George S. Patton's nickname surgically summed up the respect his allies and the fear his enemies had for World War II's most controversial general. But they only saw part of the controversy. Beneath the steely-eyed, stern face of a fighter known for verbally assaulting allies, physically slapping shell-shocked soldiers, and thumping Nazi units across North Africa, Sicily, and Europe beat the heart of a mystic. Patton believed in reincarnation and credited the ghosts of his ancestors for his courage in battle.

During World War I, the same general who later threatened soldiers for their cowardice found himself immobilized with fear in the heat of battle.

General George S. Patton, circa 1943.

Historians say that as the battle roared around Patton, he stayed in the trench until the ghosts of his grandfather—Civil War hero George Smith Patton—and several of his uncles—including his great-uncle Waller T. Patton, who was killed in Gettysburg after being wounded during Pickett's Charge—appeared to him. The ghosts of his ancestors were not happy about Patton's refusal to fight and urged him to charge out of the trench and into the melee.

It wasn't Patton's last ghostly visit from his ancestors. Historians say that during World War I, Patton was leading—on foot—a group of tanks across the battlefield, when a German machine gun bullet slashed across his leg. Patton fell into a crater, where he remained for hours before he could be rescued and evacuated. As he lay in the ditch, his ancestors returned to him again. This time they looked pleased at his gallantry and sacrifice.

During campaigns, particularly in North Africa and Sicily, Patton often surprised his assistants when he took them on impromptu tours of historic sites. The general's intimate knowledge of various ancient battlefields could be unsettling. When they asked how he knew so much about the battle, or what text he'd read to gain such clear understanding of history, Patton replied—easy, he was there when it happened. He believed that in past lives he had campaigned with Caesar, Hannibal, Alexander the Great, and—more recently—Napoleon.

Patton's campaign in this present incarnation came to an end after a vehicle accident on December 8, 1945, shortly after the war ended. Patton died in his sleep days later, on December 21.

His tenacious spirit did not give any ground, however. According to several members of his family, Patton returned in ghostly form to make sure his daughters were well. At approximately the same time of the general's death, both of Patton's daughters claimed their father visited them. His youngest daughter, Ruth Ellen, woke up and saw her dad standing at the foot of her bed. Always the impressive dresser, Patton appeared to Ruth Ellen in full military dress uniform.

"I sat up in bed — I could see him plainly. When he saw I was looking at him he gave me the sweetest smile I've ever seen," Ruth Ellen said. She was convinced that her father visited her.

The event so moved Ruth Ellen that she immediately telephoned her sister, Beatrice. Beatrice told her sister that their beloved father did not appear to her, but he reached out in a far more strange way. According to Beatrice, she was in a deep sleep when the phone by her bed rang, startling her. Phone calls at night are never a good thing, especially when your father is in a war zone. When Beatrice picked up the phone and said hello, she was relieved to hear the voice of her father crackling in considerable static. He said, "Little Bee, are you alright?"

The call—sadly and unexpectedly—broke off.

Figuring it was just a bad overseas connection, she immediately called the operator, hoping that he or she could recon-
nect them. Beatrice was shocked at the operator's answer.
Not only could the operator not connect her, but there had
been no overseas call placed. It was as if the call came out of,
well, heaven.

The two events were too much for the girls, who believed
it was not a coincidence. They believed that their father, who
never feared breaking through the line of the enemy, broke
through the final line—the one between life and death—to
communicate with his beloved family one last time.

Five-Star Ghost: Dwight D. Eisenhower

General Dwight D. Eisenhower was not as flashy as General
George Patton, or as strategically brilliant as General Douglas MacArthur, but he got the job done without making a lot
of waves. He was a blue-collar, roll up your sleeves kind of
military leader. And his soldiers loved him for that.

Eisenhower, of course, left an indelible mark on history,
both as a military and political leader. But according to
numerous witnesses and paranormal investigators, he left
more than just a mark. They have encountered his spirit in
places that might not shock you—his former residence, for
example—as well as other spots that may be a surprise, like
inside an old train.

Before the D-Day invasion, Eisenhower toured England
incessantly, making sure the equipment, facilities, and men

were preparing for the looming invasion date. At times, it seemed as if the general was supposed to be in two places at once. The travels throughout the English countryside required something speedy and safe for transport. The answer came in the form of a heavily protected train consisting of eleven cars that could tote Eisenhower, much of his staff, and even several command vehicles. In case of attack, the train's metal shutters could be closed electronically.

Some of Eisenhower's most important decisions were made on this train, and his most important directives were written there as well. A lot of his D-Day planning took place on the road—or, actually, on the rails.

General Dwight D. Eisenhower eating a C ration in Tunisia, circa 1943.

The Great Western Railway train and a London and North Eastern Railway sleeping car were included in the train. Two of the cars in Eisenhower's train, nicknamed the "Bayonet I" and "Bayonet II," became part of a famous display at the National Railroad Museum in Green Bay, Wisconsin.

Many paranormal investigators suggest that high emotional intensity can radiate into the nearby objects and very space where charged events take place. Visitors and staff of the National Railroad Museum say that you don't have to look far to prove this hypothesis. The Eisenhower display is proof.

People have said that while they were on the car they felt the presence of someone with them, even when many were completely alone at the time. Others have had more chilling encounters with whatever supernatural forces stalk the railroad museum. They say they have turned around to exit one of Eisenhower's cars and had the door slam in their faces. When they tugged at the door, they found themselves locked in!

In *Haunted Green Bay*, author Timothy Freiss writes that a volunteer at the museum was vacuuming the carpet in the Bayonet II. He was about halfway through the job when he noticed that it was time for lunch. After turning the vacuum off, he exited the car and locked the door behind him. About an hour or so later, the volunteer came back, but the instant he walked into the room he realized something was horribly wrong. He had left the vacuum cleaner in the middle of the floor, still plugged in. Now, not only was the cord unplugged and neatly rolled up, but the machine itself was rolled to the end of the room. Another weird thing: the considerable track marks the vacuum cleaner had made in the carpet had disappeared. The worker remembered a detail of a story he heard: Eisenhower was a bit of a neat freak and despised track marks in the carpet. He would often hand brush the marks out of the carpet.

The volunteer gathered up his colleagues and asked them if they had entered the train car while he was on his lunch break. Not only were his fellow volunteers nowhere near the car at the time of the incident, but they reminded the now-spooked worker that he was the only one who had a key to the car—and that key had been in his pocket the whole time.

After numerous encounters like this, the museum staff called in official ghosthunting groups. One team of paranormal investigators—Midwestern Paranormal Investigative (MPI) Network—documented their exploration of the site on the group's website. After an extensive investigation, the team concluded that the museum and especially Eisenhower's train cars were highly active, paranormally speaking. They experienced a range of phenomena and gathered quite a bit of evidence, the online report states.

Based on the evidence gathered throughout this investigation, it is the opinion of the MPI Network that the National Railroad Museum is highly active with paranormal activity. Although there's nothing definitive to indicate that General Eisenhower is the spirit that haunts the railroad cars, the team does say that the audio and visual evidence suggests that there is spirit activity present and that the spirits don't seem to be malicious. In fact, the activity was generally labeled *playful*. At times, the team felt the ghosts were just appreciative that people were reaching out to them.

While Ike's ghost may still like to go mobile in his steel-wheeled command cars, there's allegedly a part of him that is still very much a homebody, or maybe an astral homebody. According to Mark Nesbitt and Patty A. Wilson, authors of *The Big Book of Pennsylvania Ghost Stories*, reports from rangers and others who frequent Eisenhower's former farm in Gettysburg suggest that the general and former president—and possibly his wife, Mamie—is very attached to his old spread.

Eisenhower purchased the old dairy farm, now a national historic site and close to the Confederate side of the Gettysburg battlefield, because he loved the area—and the history of the area—since he was a cadet at West Point. He and another famous World War II general, Omar Bradley, spent three days in Gettysburg studying the battle as cadets at the military academy. When his service to his country as general and president was finally fulfilled, Eisenhower returned to Gettysburg for a quiet retirement to work on his memoirs.

Because the farmhouse is so old and built so close to a battlefield that bore witness to thousands of casualties and calamities, it's natural to speculate whether the property was haunted before the Eisenhowers resided there. It's also worth wondering whether Ike and Mamie themselves had any supernatural run-ins with the famous ghosts of Gettysburg. If they did, they never told anyone, and nothing appears in the general's memoirs. However, after Dwight died in 1969 and Mamie died in 1979, the National Park Service converted the farm into the Eisenhower National Historic Site, and that's when the ghost stories began to roll in. These stories came from reliable sources, too—the park rangers who are sworn to guard and maintain the property.

According to the rangers' accounts, the activity normally heats up at the end of the day and into the night. In one encounter, two rangers were in the home at night and they heard the sound of doors slamming from a bedroom. They didn't immediately think burglars had entered the property, though. The rangers had heard stories that massive, mirrored doors often slammed shut without explanation. When they arrived at the rooms in question, they didn't see any intruders. The doors had seemingly shut all by themselves. The rangers weren't given to believing in spooks and superstitions, so they tried to debunk the event. One suggested it was the wind, but the doors were too heavy. And the wind would have to be pretty strong and concentrated to close sliding doors and not touch anything else in the room.

In another case, rangers were in the home during a cold February night. One was in the kitchen when he heard the unmistakable sounds of someone walking down the back stairs. He figured it was his colleague coming down to check on him. He called out to her. But there was no answer, so he went to find the source of these steps. Something else was going on. He claimed that soon after he heard the steps, he felt a presence, as if someone was in the room with him—watching him. Eventually, he found his colleague, but she was far from where he heard the footsteps. They both split up and searched the home—but found no one.

By the time the search was complete and they were satisfied that the house was empty, the two rangers decided to lock up and leave for the evening. As they both stood in the living room, they both heard the same footfalls, gently making their way down the carpeted stairs.

It takes a lot to rattle rangers, but the second incident was enough to make both rangers dart out the door and lock it safely behind them.

In yet another case, a ranger said that on the anniversary of Ike's death—March 28—she heard someone coughing. It sounded like someone was in the butler's quarters. But the second she stood at the entry to the room, the coughing stopped. As she entered, she saw the room was vacant.

This is just some of the phenomena. The authors write that people have heard the ringing of servant bells and the rustle of gowns. Another employee, after locking up and leaving the premises, claimed to see the shade of Mamie's bedroom lift purposefully and then fall, as if someone was in the room, making sure all the visitors were gone.

Prime Minister of the Paranormal: Winston Churchill

No single human being reflected the indomitable spirit of the English people quite like Winston Churchill. Solid—if not a little out of shape—and bulldog-faced, Churchill showed no sign of fear as he faced down the steel wall of panzers and iron cloud of Messerschmitts flooding Europe. He would not back down—and neither would the British people.

*Prime Minister Winston Churchill
reviews Polish troops in England, circa 1943.*

The former English prime minister still won't release his grip on his beloved homeland, according to the many people who claim to have seen Churchill's ghost. Others say they smell him, or at least his cigar.

Tour guides of haunted London always stop by the official residence that has long served as home to British prime ministers and a hub of the nation's government—Number 10 Downing Street. They say that Churchill's spirit is part of the ghostly tapestry that shrouds the building. Several people say they smell the unmistakable odor of cigar smoke in certain areas of the home. They are certain that it's old Winston smoking on a stogie.

Other times, the former British prime minister shows up in the most unlikely of places, like a London subway.

According to a story in the *Daily Mirror*, a visitor to London was in the London Underground waiting to take the train—or the Tube—to his hotel. Craig Cooper told the paper he was overcome with the feeling that a presence was nearby. In fact, the presence was right next to him. But it was midnight and he was all alone in the Queensway Station. There was no one else around.

Cooper said he felt like someone was standing right behind him. Because his girlfriend back home had never traveled on London's famous subway system, he was already snapping some pictures. When he got back to his hotel room, he decided to review the photos he took. In one picture, taken around the time that he started to feel a presence in the Tube station, he could make out the frosty image of a man—a man who looked just like the former prime minister of England. Since there was no one else in the station at the time, he couldn't come up with any other explanation. Many of his friends and family who saw it also admitted that the visage of Winston Churchill was definitely noticeable in the digital photo.

What Cooper did not know was that the very spot where he snapped the phantom photo was the location in the London Underground that Churchill used frequently during the war. In fact, the location of what's now a busy station for commuters was used as a bunker to keep the prime minister safe as Nazi bombs rained down on the city. It's conveniently located close to Hyde Park, World War II experts note. During the war, with nearly every citizen taking part in the war effort in some way, this area bustled with intense physical, mental, and, perhaps, spiritual activity. According to paranormal theorists, some of that energy remains, making it an ideal place for ghosts to manifest.

In fact, Cooper's supernatural experience—and the resulting photographic evidence—is nothing new for the area. Although Queensway Station remained quiet for a few decades, in the 1980s it was a hotspot for paranormal encounters, including ones that involved the ghost of Churchill.

Since the sighting, Cooper's picture has been debated. One camp says the photo simply shows the light reflecting off the flooring. Others say it's more than a coincidence when flooring takes the shape of a famous prime minister. Still others say that it would make sense for Winston to visit his old stomping and cigar-chomping grounds. They say the prime minister was a great believer in the supernatural. He said he was convinced of the supernatural because of the numerous miraculous interventions—especially during the Boer War—that had saved his life.

An overnight stay in a haunted bedroom at the White House during World War II may have convinced him even more.

According to historians, Churchill may have had a paranormal encounter with another of history's great wartime leaders. This leader, like Churchill, had been severely tested by the winds of war and had felt the awesome weight of responsibility for the lives of millions of soldiers and citizens.

According to Churchill's account, it was none other than the ghost of the Great Emancipator—Abraham Lincoln—who appeared to him while he was staying at the White House. Apparently he saw Lincoln's ghost while engaging in one of many favorite peculiarities—walking around naked.

Churchill said that he was staying in the Lincoln bedroom at the White House on an official visit during the war. The bedroom wasn't his favorite B & B in the capital, he admitted. But in any event, he decided to take a nice, long, evening bath and retire for the rest of the night. He finished his bath and strolled out of the bathroom and into the bedroom's main area—completely naked, but still clutching his trademark cigar. As he walked into the room, Churchill said he saw the nearly transparent ghost of Abraham Lincoln standing by the fireplace.

He said that Lincoln looked directly at him. We have no way of knowing of what expression formed on Lincoln's face after witnessing the sight of the naked, corpulent prime minister in his bedroom, but Churchill maintained his composure.

The prime minister supposedly looked right at Lincoln and said, "Good evening, Mr. President. You seem to have me at a disadvantage."

With that, Churchill said Lincoln smiled at him and slowly faded away.

As we said, Churchill was open to the supernatural. But that doesn't mean he encouraged these encounters. Reports say he refused to stay in the Lincoln bedroom again. And after seeing Churchill naked, Lincoln might not mind the prime minister's sleight.

A German General's Ghost in America: Erwin Rommel

He appeared like a phantom—or an angel of death—without warning and without mercy.

He was in front of them. Behind them. On the right flank. On the left flank.

This mysterious force swept through eastern Europe, then smashed through France, and then, just as a perfect predator adapts to any environment, he mastered the desert and turned North Africa into a killing zone. The name of this wizard of war haunted the Allied forces: Erwin Rommel. However, he was better known as "the Desert Fox," a nickname that reflected his stealthy military genius and the fear he spread among the Allied ranks. Perhaps it also hinted at the respect and—dare I say—admiration that soldiers on both sides had for Rommel.

The German general who had vanquished nearly every enemy in front of him finally fell, not on the field of battle, but in a net of political intrigue when his involvement in the plot to kill Adolf Hitler became known to the Führer himself. He was told to commit suicide or face the grim torture and execution of the other plotters. Wanting to spare his family that embarrassment, Rommel committed suicide. As with other warriors whom we have studied in this volume, the general may be gone, but his spirit cannot rest. While it might not surprise you that the ghost of the Desert Fox continues to haunt legendary battlefields, you might be surprised by where exactly Rommel's ghost has appeared and which battlefields his spirit stalks. Rommel ghost stories are centered not in Europe or North Africa, but in the United States. And he's been seen lurking not in the battlefields of World War II, but areas more closely associated with the American Civil War.

In our first story, several witnesses who have traveled to the Mount Hebron Cemetery say that the graveyard is haunted. And why wouldn't it be? The cemetery is located in the Winchester, Virginia, area and serves as the final resting place of some famous Americans, including markers for Civil War heroes George and Tazewell Patton. The Patton brothers gained fame for their actions during the Civil War, as Confederate leaders. George gained more fame by becoming the grandfather of World War II general George S. Patton.

On some nights, visitors walking through the cemetery say they see a strange sight. A man in a long gray coat and a cap appears to be silently standing alone over the Pattons' graves. He doesn't move. He doesn't speak. He seems lost in thought. Some of the braver souls try to approach the figure, but say he walks away—or fades away—before they can reach the spot. Stories about this strange sighting started right after World War II, local occult historians say.

But why would a German general haunt an American cemetery?

It's a good question.

These same historians have an unusual theory to explain the haunting. They believe the ghost is none other than Field Marshall Erwin Rommel paying his respects to the Confederate dead, whom Rommel considered heroes for their individual valor and military prowess. They say back in the 1930s, Rommel and a few other German generals slipped into the United States to tour American Civil War battlefields. In particular, they were tracing the footsteps of

General Thomas "Stonewall" Jackson and General Nathan Bedford Forrest, two military geniuses who served as early pioneers of lightning-quick, audacious maneuvering military tactics that later become the keystones of Germany's blitzkrieg style of warfare. Remember: Winchester and the Shenandoah valley were scenes of some of Jackson's most well-known maneuvers. Perhaps, the legend suggests, Rommel still feels kinship with the military leaders of a bygone era, maybe more so than his German colleagues, with whom he had a fatal falling-out at the end of the war.

But this is complete speculation. Historians—and even historians and biographers who specialize in Rommel—say there's no evidence that the German general ever visited the United States, let alone the Shenandoah valley.

The believers in the legend have a counter: Perhaps Rommel and his comrades came to the United States under the strictest secrecy. They did not wish to give the American military any hints that they were plotting offensive action and using Americans history as a how-to guide! The visit, therefore, could risk an international incident, the believers suggest. They also point to another ghost story as evidence that Rommel made his way to the states for a pre-war study session.

Another stop on Rommel's alleged tour of America was the Highland Inn in the western highlands of Virginia. Its strategic proximity to several key battles of the Civil War could not have been lost on Rommel's keen military mind. According to a legend that has been spreading since the

1950s, Rommel stayed at the inn under an assumed name for about three weeks, while he studied Stonewall Jackson's maneuvers. The hotel management asks that you take that legend with a grain of salt. There's no historical proof of this happening, either.

While there doesn't seem to be historical evidence, a lot of people believe there is some paranormal evidence. Witnesses claim they haven't seen Rommel's ghost, but they have smelled the scent of pipe smoke wafting around the balcony. They claim this is where the general came to take a few puffs of his pipe while he studied and contemplated the tactics and strategies of America's most creative military minds—minds that may have stirred the first notions of blitzkrieg in Rommel's fertile imagination.

Pipe smoke and the feeling that someone is nearby might just be coincidences or runaway imaginations, say some skeptics, who keep pointing to the lack of historical evidence.

It's a debate that Rommel, a master of deception and disguise, would find particularly ironic.

5

MAGIC BATTLES, MYSTIC WARRIORS, AND PSYCHIC WARFARE

Everyone knows the history. The Allies won World War II on the beaches and in the fields, on the streets and in the hills, just as Winston Churchill promised during the dark days of 1940 when the conflict was far from decided. They won it in the air and on the high seas. They fought with tanks, ships, planes, and the sheer fighting will of the individual soldier.

But did the Allies also win the war in secret meeting halls and around sacred fires, as they unleashed wizards and witches, occultists and magicians, and even positive thinking on the Axis powers? And what powers were these

Allied occultists up against? Did the Nazis marshal their own magical forces into this battle?

The answers may surprise you. And the names of those soldiers involved in that fight may shock you even more.

We head to the magical front lines now.

Crowley and Hitler: Battle of the Beasts

We'll start our history of the magical battles that were waged to win World War II with the most improbable alliance within the Allied war effort. Among the white witches and black magicians who enlisted to spiritually fight Germany and her Axis partners was at least one notorious letch who bragged about being the Antichrist, and a famous intelligence officer turned literary master, who gave us one of the world's most enduring movie spies.

To find the roots of this unlikely spy team, you have to remember that if politics makes strange bedfellows, war makes the strangest bedfellows conceivable. At least the men who would make up World War II's strangest alliance—Aleister Crowley, an occultist and founder of a religion called Thelema, and Ian Fleming, creator of James Bond—had somewhat similar beginnings. Both were born in wealthy aristocratic English homes—Crowley in the late nineteenth century and Fleming in the early twentieth century. Both sowed quite a field of wild oats during their youth in some of England's finest schools. Both were drawn to writing.

But the similarities ended there.

Fleming eventually bowed to the pressures of his aristocratic family and tied down a series of respectable jobs, including positions in banking and journalism. Crowley never bowed to anyone or anything. He held a series of disrespectable titles, including sexual libertine, cult leader, and ceremonial magician, jobs that soon drew the attention and then ire of Britain's Victorian Age press. The reporters and editors—and for all we know, Fleming himself—referred to Crowley as "the wickedest man in the world." Crowley enjoyed the moniker, but did them one better by calling himself "the Beast." He relished his role as England's number one vote-getter for most likely to be the Antichrist.

Not exactly known for running in the same circles—or pentagrams—it's unlikely that Fleming and Crowley would have ever crossed paths. That all changed when the winds of war began to whip the British Isles and the Axis powers threatened the shores with invasion. Crowley, like the long lineage of England's magicians and wizards starting with Merlin, became quite the patriot—and propagandist—when push came to shove. He asked to work with the British intelligence, but the request was formally declined. We'll use the term *formally* because, as we will see, there are at least a few experts who believe that the occultist did work for the intelligence service, and with Fleming specifically. They suggest that because the mission was so clandestine, the intelligence community refused to officially recognize that Crowley joined the group as their most secret—as in occult—agent. Officially, Crowley, always a bit of a bard, wrote poems that served as propaganda for the Allied cause. One poem, "La Gauloise" (Song of the Free French), was even sent to the headquarters of the Free French—the French government in exile—where the group's leader, General Charles de Gaulle, reportedly praised his work.

But it was more than his wordsmithing that helped out the Allies the most, according to several experts on Crowley's war efforts. It was also his spellcrafting.

The story goes that members of the intelligence community, including, perhaps, Fleming himself, were interested in countering the Third Reich's own occult operations with an Allied supernatural assault. As will be discussed in more detail throughout this volume, many in the Nazi party were rumored to be involved in the occult. In fact, the Nazi party itself could be seen as a wild offshoot of a German occult movement. Hitler, or at least his associates, joined as members of the Thule Society, which mixed racist Aryan ideology with occult theories. One of those Nazi occult believers soon walked dead center into Crowley's magical crosshairs.

Rudolf Hess was among Hitler's oldest and most trusted comrades. He was right next to Hitler on November 8, 1923, when the Nazis' ill-fated coup, called the Beer Hall Putsch, fell apart. Hess also helped the Führer write his diabolical classic, *Mein Kampf*, while both served time in prison for their role in the coup.

As the Nazis first seized and then consolidated political power in Germany, Hitler appointed Hess deputy führer. Historians consider him the third most powerful man in the Third Reich, after Hitler himself, and Luftwaffe master, Herman Goering. According to some historians, Hess was also arguably the most powerful occultist in the Nazi leadership circle. While some historians are not sure about the depth of certain Nazi occult leanings, most agree that Hess joined the Thule Society and was a firm believer in prophecy, astrology, and occult powers.

Whether Fleming believed in the same magical powers as Crowley and Hess or just looked at Hess's beliefs as weak points that could be manipulated is not known, but the soon-to-be James Bond author and the British intelligence community deemed the Nazi deputy führer a vulnerable target in the occult theater of war. Fleming also knew the UK had a secret weapon: Aleister Crowley.

Fleming reportedly reached out to Crowley to find a way to contact Hess, according to several sources. His reasoning was simple: Crowley was a well-known occultist and Hess was enthralled by the occult. If Crowley could communicate with Hess, perhaps he could convince the deputy führer that he was receiving astrological predictions about the Third Reich. The English intelligence officers could then manipulate the astrological forecasts to trick Hess into doing their bidding, all to the detriment of the Nazi cause.

Crowley did his intelligence handlers one better. Instead of merely reaching out to Hess, Crowley would bring the deputy führer to them.

Shortly after Fleming and Crowley discussed the idea of contacting Hess, England's supernatural special forces master sprang into action. Crowley went into seclusion, preparing a spell that would summon the Nazi leader to the UK. Crowley later bragged that within days of casting this spell, Hess, an aviation buff, commandeered a modified Messerschmitt Bf 110 and, on May 10, 1941, pointed the craft toward the United Kingdom, supposedly on a mission to broker peace between the two countries.

According to *Smithsonian* magazine, Albert Speer, the Nazi architect who was jailed with Hess, suggested that Hess's account of why he made the flight matches up with Crowley's.

"Hess assured me in all seriousness that the idea had been inspired in him in a dream by supernatural forces," Speer said. "We will guarantee England her empire; in return she will give us a free hand in Europe."

After the thousand-mile flight from Bavaria, he parachuted into Scotland and landed in a town near Glasgow— right next to an angry, patriotic Scottish farmer armed with a pitchfork, according to one version of the story. The pitchfork-armed patriot turned the German aviator over to authorities, who soon found out that their new POW was a Nazi VIP.

Of course, maybe they already knew, because Crowley and Fleming had told them to expect a visitor.

Hitler, who went off the deep end faster and harder than any other figure in modern history, *really* went off the deep end after Hess's decision, according to most accounts. He screamed and ranted about Hess's betrayal—and then moved into action.

Officially, Nazi spin doctors claimed that Hess had become mentally unstable and that his actions were nothing more than an idiotic plan.

Hitler's other actions, however, showed just who the Führer really blamed. Police decisively rounded up fortune tellers, religious leaders, faith healers and, ostensibly, anyone who may have had occult leanings. Perhaps Hitler thought these weak-minded frauds made his regime vulnerable to psychological manipulation from the Allies. On the other hand, Hitler may have been convinced that some magical force wielded by mysterious occultists actually did prompt Hess's deranged airplane ride. Like a modern version of baby-killing Herod, Hitler sought to snuff out any magical opposition by killing anyone who might have such powers.

In any event, safely across the English Channel, the Allies' master magician—and perhaps the very one who stirred Hess's flight—remained untouched by Hitler's paranormal purge and was free to weave his martial magic at will. Accounts differ, but there are some historians and a lot of occult experts who believe that Crowley personally interrogated Hess at Fleming's behest. After all, the now ex-Nazi leader was impressed—or, better yet, intimidated—by the Beast's reputation. There's no conclusive historical proof that Crowley helped out on shaking down Hess for information, however.

Fleming's invitation to Crowley to help him interrogate Hess may have been nothing more than a mere gesture to enlist England's biggest occult master in the war effort, but it was *Crowley's* gesture that may have reversed both Nazi curses and turned the Axis tide.

We know that gesture better as the peace sign, or possibly the *V for victory* sign.

But Crowley knew it as a magical foil, a gesture that can ward off evil forces. Crowley claimed that he aimed his two-fingered salute at diminishing the evil powers of the Nazis' swastika, an ancient magical symbol, and the Germans' infamous stiff outstretched arm salute, which some occult experts also believe was actually a ritualistic gesture.

According to Crowley, he used his own connections in the British Broadcasting Corporation (BBC) and British intelligence to pass on his idea for the magical gesture. He also stated that the idea made its way to the highest reaches of England's wartime government, eventually reaching Prime Minister Winston Churchill, who not only approved the sign, but became synonymous with its use.

As proof, he pointed to his own published book of magick—a 1913 volume that featured both the V for victory sign and the swastika. As further proof, Crowley would no doubt point to the increasing string of defeats that Nazi forces were suffering on the battlefield.

The peace sign, in the end, bested the swastika.

Witches United: How England's Witches and Wiccans United to Stop Hitler

While Aleister Crowley used his magic power to drain Hitler's brain trust and countered the evil power of Nazi symbolism with a two-fingered salute, dozens of other supernaturally empowered British citizens were taking positions to keep England safe and ensure that the German's pending Operation Sea Lion—the plan to invade the UK—never left the shores of France.

There are at least three accounts of England's magical forces mustering to defeat the Nazis. Like any account of supernatural intervention, the facts are hard to tease out from the myth, but in the pages ahead we will read about the ritualistic bulldog response that England's witches, wizards, sorcerers, and spiritual followers had on Germany's threats to land troops on England's shores.

Gerald Gardner, a pioneer in the pagan religious movement we know as Wicca, says that covens of witches turned out to magically battle Hitler's armies in the middle part of 1940, a particularly bleak time for England's war efforts.

The Nazis swarmed into France and installed the puppet Vichy regime. The Luftwaffe also began its air attacks on the United Kingdom and German troops even occupied some of England's Channel Islands.

Gardner said that covens of witches convened on July 31, 1940, in southern England, right before the Nazi invasion was supposedly ordered to begin. If Gardner's estimations are right—and if the witches' convention even happened at all—it would rank among the largest gatherings of magical practitioners in modern history.

The group that gathered in a section of New Forest, one of the last remaining tracts of open space and pastureland left in the increasingly urbanized southern England, was massive, according to Gardner. However, he never gave hard numbers on how many witches and warlocks joined him in what he referred to as Operation Cone of Power. He did say, however, that the magical energy they put off was so massive that he could feel the intensity like he had been hit by a wind gust or he had just touched a live wire. It was palpable.

Besides the sheer number of practitioners, Gardner said the witches had another advantage. The New Forest coven, which spearheaded this magical assault, was among the most ancient and most powerful covens in Europe. It could trace its lineage directly back to pre-Christian times, an era when people respected witches as elders and healers in the community. They had a lot of experience dealing with invaders.

While millions of other Englishmen were being recruited for the pending war in Europe, Gardner said that English witches called him up as a soldier in the magic war. He said one of England's most powerful magicians initiated him into the New Forest coven. Although she is often referred to as Dorothy Clutterbuck or Old Dorothy Clutterbuck, the name may be a pseudonym, or, according to critics, she may have just been one of Gardner's inside jokes. There actually was a Dorothy Clutterbuck who lived about the time Gardner claimed to be initiated, but experts who read the woman's diaries and personal papers agree she seemed to have no connection with the occult, let alone the New Forest coven.

Joke or not, Gardner's story is that he met Old Dorothy one September evening in 1939, right before the war started. Old Dorothy then required the initiate to strip naked and participate in a ritual. Gardner's initiation revealed that his scholarly journey to discover whether elements of the ancient Wicca religion still existed was well-founded. His ultimate destiny as a promoter of the religion was also reportedly revealed during the initiation. Gardner became nearly synonymous with the founding of Wicca and modern witchcraft.

According to Gardner, the witches from the New Forest coven, as well as other covens throughout the country, gathered at night and formed the "great circle." They then formed the cone of power, which, as the magician described it, generated a great vortex of magical energy. Gardner said that once the energy reached its peak, the combined force of witches aimed it at Berlin with the verbal instructions, "You cannot cross the sea, you cannot cross the sea, you cannot come, you cannot come."

Gardner and a few other occult experts say that the energy given off by the group was incredibly powerful—or, you could say, deadly. They reported a few casualties—some of the coven members and participants died later. Some were stricken with pneumonia and were unable to fight off the disease because of their weakened immune systems. Others died of heart failure.

Skeptics and believers will debate whether these deaths had anything to do with the witches' participation in the gathering at New Forest or not. But history is emphatic that the Nazis, who were up to their swastika armbands and epaulettes with hubris after blitzkrieging through Poland and France, ran into a series of misfortunes and miscalculations that made the short hop from the north of France into England nearly impossible. England's pilots beat back the air war. The German navy, with all its sneaky submarine U-boats, could not minimize the destructive power of the Royal Navy. Some historians even say Hitler was afraid of the sea and began to lose his nerve. He had once told his naval officers, "On land, I am a hero. At sea, I am a coward."

The spell may have had one final, disastrous effect on the Nazi regime. With the door to England closed by aircraft, naval craft, and witchcraft, Hitler turned his war machine toward Russia, a final and fatal decision. The attack on the USSR depleted precious sources and made a two-front war nearly unavoidable.

The question remains: Did that historic slide begin as a circle of wizards and witches gathered in the forests of England?

By the way, you might think this story sounds oddly familiar, like the plot of the classic movie *Bedknobs and Broomsticks.* That's because there are indications that Gardner and Old Dorothy served as inspirations for at least some of the movie.

Dion Fortune

Another one of the magic warriors whom the Allies drafted was Dion Fortune.

According to Gareth Knight, writing in *The Magical Battle of Britain*, Fortune might have been one of the earliest practitioners of psychotherapy. But she felt it didn't go far enough to explain things like telepathy and other forms of psychic powers. Her background in psychology and parapsychology made her keenly aware of the existence of a group mind. She recognized that the British citizens created a group mind, and that it existed as England's greatest strength, as well as its most vulnerable target. Nazi propaganda and black magic was aimed directly at that group mind and she vowed to protect it.

During World War II, Fortune rallied her troops with a continual barrage of letters designed to steel their hearts and lift their spirits, the perfect condition for magic to happen.

She sent her first letter in October of 1939. The simple message—a kind of "keep calm and magic on" type of thing—arrived in the postal boxes of members of the Fraternity of Inner Light, a group she led. That message came right on time, as waves of Nazi bombers and fighter planes soared over British skies. It wasn't exactly a time brimming with confidence. In fact, a spirit of gloom had taken over England and much of the west. Some might say it was a terrible time to test one's belief in magic, but Fortune and others would suggest it was the perfect time because it was completely necessary.

The letters also invoked creative visualization exercises to accomplish their aims. She asked her members to visualize angelic protectors who were keeping England safe and their morale strong.

Fortune included specific steps for meditation. This may have violated some of the group's and her own principles. These visualization and meditation efforts magnified considerable spiritual power, forces that might turn harmful. Still, desperate times called for desperate magical measures.

The following comes from the letters printed in *The Magical Battle of Britain*: "Let us meditate upon angelic Presences, red-robed and armed, patrolling the length and breadth of our land. Visualise a map of Great Britain, and picture these great Presences moving as a vast shadowy form along the coasts, and backwards and forwards from north to south and east to west, keeping watch and ward so that nothing alien can move unobserved."

Stripping this down to its most essential element, the practice was based on a well-established occult principle, "As above, so below," or, less esoterically, consciousness creates conditions. If the practitioners dwelled—heart, mind, and soul—on victory and peace, that's what would happen.

With members scattered across the nation, some of whom were involved in the war effort, Fortune established regularly timed meditation sessions. Groups or individuals would try to meet every Sunday at the same time and in the same place. Participants who could not make the meeting were expected to participate in the ritual wherever they found themselves at the time—in a bunker spotting aircraft, in barracks, at home, wherever. This concentrated effort, she hoped, would help magnify the results of their attempts.

Fortune told them the visualizations and rituals made additional lines of defense, not the sole line of defense. "The war has to be fought and won on the physical plane before physical manifestation can be given to the archetypal ideals," Fortune wrote.

For Fortune, the collective magical effort during the war ended up, ironically, creating a long-term benefit. She remembers almost wistfully, "Those who were with us in those days will remember how we opened our doors and welcomed all who would sit in meditation with us and taught them the esoteric methods of mind-working that had never been revealed before outside the Veil of Mysteries, and that this work was done with a view to bringing into manifestation those very ideas that are now manifesting. What part we played in their manifestation we cannot know; but we do know that whereas then the Fraternity was a voice crying in the wilderness, the cry has now become a chorus."

The Allies were fortunate to have such a trained psychic warrior on their side. She claimed that she was a victim of a psychic attack as a young woman and immediately wrote a manual on how to survive such an attack, titled *Psychic Self-Defense*.

What she may not have known at that time was that this guide—a primer on self-defense against occult powers—would position her, you might say, as the UK's "minister of psychic defense" during this worldwide struggle against the greatest occult force of the modern era, the Nazi regime.

US Marshals Its Spiritual Forces

The United States joined the war effort late, but when it did, the US brought the full weight of its military prowess and industrial genius to the fight. The Americans also brought another weapon into the conflict—their spiritual warriors.

As Mitch Horowitz points out in his books *Occult America* and *One Simple Idea*, while the United States is often recognized as a mainstream Christian country, the country's occult and magical practitioners have actually thrived beneath the surface of American culture. The belief systems include robust populations of Wiccans, spiritualists, positive thinkers, and many other adherents. Often pushed to the margins of mainstream religious thought and philosophy, these spiritual seekers, paradoxically, were frequent vanguards of cultural shifts and religious renewal.

During World War II, in the fight against the Axis powers, Americans relied heavily on their reliable power of prayer, but many also explored the borders of occult powers, especially in the realm of a positive thinking philosophy called New Thought. It's a philosophy steeped in faith, optimism, and self-reliance, main themes of American culture and philosophy. New Thought can trace its origins to the country's transcendentalist movement, led by philosophers like Ralph Waldo Emerson and Henry David Thoreau, and even to the works and thoughts of founding fathers like Thomas Jefferson and Benjamin Franklin. But New Thought also contains a hint of the occult.

Later, the spiritualist movement—which brought mediums and communing with spirits in séances into the American mainstream—probed for a deeper interaction between mind and matter, spirit and destiny.

Frank B. Robinson, often referred to as the "Mail-Order Prophet," was one of those spiritual warriors sculpted from the same American metaphysical material as Emerson and Thoreau. Robinson, originally from England and a former Bible school student who rejected organized religion, formed his own New Thought group, called Psychiana, based in Moscow, Idaho. He believed in the power of prayer and affirmations. And like any good prophet, Robinson even claimed he talked to God.

His most powerful weapon, though, was a thorough understanding of one of the most occult forces at work in America: marketing. Long before televangelists and e-commerce, Robinson used advertising and mail-order to spread the message of Psychiana.

Horowitz writes, "As Psychiana grew, Robinson kept up with thousands of correspondents who wrote him with personal questions or requests for prayer. The Idaho town's tiny post-office was flooded with letters—sometimes postmarked no more than 'Psychiana, U.S.A.' or 'Doctor Robinson, Idaho' or even 'The Man Who Talked With God, Idaho.'"

When World War II broke out, Robinson used both the power of mind and the power of marketing to enlist his group members to join the fray, using their psychic powers to defeat the Nazi and Japanese powers. He actually had experience dealing with fascists. Before the war, the mail-order minister's mind power message connected with an unlikely student. Italian dictator Benito Mussolini sent Robinson a letter praising Psychiana.

Robinson wasn't exactly a fan of his, though.

When the conflict started, the prophet from Moscow, Idaho, attempted to sway his fascist fan from embarking on a war that would engulf the world. He publicly chided Mussolini, telling him to "refrain from joining Hitler in his crusade of madness."

The message was never answered.

But the cold shoulder from Il Duce did not cause Robinson to shirk from battling the forces of fascism. He turned Psychiana into an army against them, calling on his followers to become "A Blitzkrieg for God." Horowitz said that Robinson sent group members buttons with Hitler's image on it. On the button was a magic spell that read, "I am helping to bring Hitler's defeat by repeating hourly: the power of Right (God) will bring your speedy downfall."

Robinson reached out to other allies facing the Nazi onslaught. He sent a message to Finland's leaders, saying that Psychiana members would join Finnish cabinet and military members for fifteen-minute affirmation sessions. During those sessions they would affirm: "The power of God is superior to the powers of war, hate, and evil."

The prime minister of the country during the war, Risto Ryti, replied that they were prepared to enact the suggestion.

Robinson knew that he and his Psychiana troops couldn't change the tide of war alone. They would need help.

He also knew that thousands of other loyal Americans who wanted to end the war were members of New Thought and mind power groups. Horowitz writes that Robinson and one of the movement's biggest names in the positive thinking philosophy joined forces to defeat the Axis powers.

Ernest Holmes, who wrote the classic New Thought text *Science of Mind*, joined Robinson's crusade against the enemy regimes as the winds of conflict whipped into World War II. The two prophets—and their 3,500 strong collective legion of followers—met at the Philharmonic Auditorium in Los Angeles in September of 1941. Although most of the world had spun out of control and into war, the United States remained on the sidelines. Holmes and Robinson, however, were preparing their team to join the fight.

Robinson called the rally the "Holmes-Robinson Spiritual Awakening"—or, at other times, "American Spiritual Awakening"—and invited all Americans to take part. Both spiritual leaders welcomed all religious beliefs and accepted people from all ethnicities and national origins, a stark contrast from the fascist enemies arrayed against the US and its allies.

In his opening remarks to the crowd, Holmes outlines this acceptance of all religions in no uncertain terms:

"Some of you may go to a Jewish Synagogue; you may be a Methodist, Baptist, Catholic, but there is but one God. We meet here today not on a theological background, but upon the foreground of a spiritual conception, the common meeting ground of every race, every creed, every color, every philosophy, and every religion on the face of the earth."

Robinson also appealed the group to realize the strength of diversity in their fight against the Nazis. When Robinson spoke, he referred to the diverse audience as "beloved."

"Now, Beloved, when the Almighty created the human race, He created black, white, yellow, and every other color which exists on earth, in one creation. He did not make three or four special jobs of creation, nor did he make several different attributes, one for each nation. He made them all flesh and blood—every human soul that has ever lived on the face of this earth. We are all brothers, regardless of our religious affiliation, our race, or nationality."

Robinson did live to see that the psychic warfare on the Axis powers was apparently successful, but, Psychiana and the power of the New Thought alliance he forged with Holmes did not play a significant role in the reconciliation and reconstruction efforts of the post-war politics. Robinson died in October, 1948. Psychiana essentially died with him.

Holmes, however, made sure that his *Science of Mind* doctrine would continue to soldier on. It is still fighting spiritual battles today.

Robinson's mind power techniques to fight against tyranny and fascism would rise again too. Paraphrasing the Mail-Order Prophet, Horowitz created his own social media campaign in 2015 to unite his readers against the terrorist group ISIS. Echoing Robinson, he posted the following on several social media outlets: "I am inaugurating the same campaign against ISIS. Please join me in adapting Frank's slogan: 'I am helping to bring about the immediate defeat of ISIS by repeating hourly: 'THE POWER OF RIGHT (GOD) WILL BRING ABOUT YOUR SPEEDY DOWNFALL.' Pass it on. #MindOverISIS."

Axis Forces: Nazi Occult Power

After nearly defeating the Allied powers in World War I, Germany's subsequent loss in World War I propelled the country into a state of economic and political ruin. According to experts on the occult, it was clearly the spiritual ruin that pushed the once world-leading, culturally refined German people to the brink of complete annihilation in World War II.

These experts on the occult suggest that Germany had become possessed.

Led by a madman who some claimed was demon-possessed himself, the Nazi party first bullied its way onto Germany's political stage and then, as if lifted by an evil wizard's spell—or, perhaps, curse—began to dominate the social, political, cultural, and even spiritual values of the country. The black-uniformed SS and the fires that burned at the Reichstag seemed more like costumes and plot lines pulled from a low-budget horror movie. And the Nazi soldiers and party leaders appeared to be more like dark arts masters involved in occult rituals than any type of governmental agency.

But were the dark arts really involved?

It's a controversial subject among historians. But it's not an argument about whether the occult influenced Nazism at all. Historians may argue about the extent of the occult, but most acknowledge that dark aspects of the occult infected the Nazi elite. But there's another debate: Did this quest for magical power have any effect on Germany's successes and failures during the war?

We'll explore this idea, as well as investigate how some Nazi leaders and philosophers were influenced by the occult, as we now peer into the weird and malevolent world of the Nazi regime.

The Rise of the Thule Society

The Nazi party itself could be seen as the bastard child of several occult movements that came into vogue during the tumultuous years between the world wars. While critics often dismiss allegations of the party's occult ties as being overdone and merely reflective of German society at large, it's difficult to imagine that the Nazi party could have formed and gained power without help and guidance from certain Germanic occult groups, especially the Thule Society. It's also difficult to imagine the Nazis not usurping the membership of these societies—when expedient—since they clearly resonated with much of their ideology.

Whether the Nazi party grew as an extension of occult groups or vice versa can be debated. What can't be debated is the extent to which these groups spread in the dark days after World War I and before the even darker days of the fascist takeover.

Several leading members of the Nazi party before Hitler's takeover in the 1930s were involved at various levels with groups such as the Thule Society. The occult group traces its origin to a disgruntled World War I veteran. Walter Nauhaus began the organization as a study group. It's probably no coincidence that the belief system he began to construct would interest leaders of the burgeoning Nazi movement. After all, both Nauhaus and the party's future leader, Adolf Hitler, were World War I vets, anti-Semitic, art students, and very bitter. Some Hitler biographers claim that Hitler joined the Thule Society, while others claim there isn't proof of that. Most historians admit that leading party members Rudolf Hess and Hans Frank were definitely members, while other Nazis may have had more informal ties to the group, such as brief speaking appearances at the group's meetings.

Still, the Thule Society's basic occult teachings must have served some purpose for the Nazis. Society members believed in a divine origin of the Aryan race, as did the Nazi Third Reich. The deep and strident anti-Semitism of the society's mythology, which portrayed the Aryans as a people betrayed by Jews, lent itself well to propaganda for Hitler and his nationalist movement, which sought a scapegoat for Germany's loss in the war and its dire economic conditions.

Thule, by the way, was the name that ancient Roman and Greek geographers used when they referred to the northern edges of the known world. In today's world, we mainly call it Scandinavia. However, for the society's members, Thule had a magical origin. They believed that Thule was an island or landmass near Greenland or Iceland. The kingdom was the original home of the Aryan race. Members also believed that Plato's tale about Atlantis actually referred to Thule.

Members must have seen the rise of Hitler and his ambitions for a Third Reich as a way to reanimate the lost kingdom of Thule.

Vril Society

Thule Society wasn't the only occult group active before Hitler's ascent. Some historians who've studied the Nazis' occult activities say that a secret group espousing racial superiority—and wielding magic power—was pulling the strings of German society, leading the country ever closer to worldwide conflagration.

But, like every occult Nazi mystery, the Vril Society (as the group is often called) is still cloaked in layers of secrecy and fraud, and wrapped in tentacles of suspicion and paranoia. In fact, the society could be nothing more than a plot twist from a work of fiction called *Vril: The Power of the Coming Race*, by Edward Bulwer-Lytton. According to this book, a master race lives within the earth and has learned how to use a mysterious force called Vril. The force gives them awesome power to heal, as well as equally astonishing power to kill and destroy.

As an allegory, the tale of the Vril-ya, or the people who possess the power of Vril, certainly sounds like the Nazi movement, which started in the substrata of society, among the outcasts and rejects of the class-conscious German culture. There was—and perhaps still are—a group of occultists who believed that this novel was a true account, not a work of fiction. They believed in the Vril-ya, their power, and a group of humans who somehow established contact with these subterranean overlords. The story of the Vril wasn't just a folk legend passed around in German villages. Some of the Vril believers were among the biggest names in the occult world at the time; people like Helena Blavatsky, founder of the Theosophy Society and Rudolf Steiner, an occult leader who would later find himself—and his alleged magical powers—in the sights of Nazi magicians.

The hard pieces of proof that believers of the Vril-Nazi connection offer are the unmatched success of German forces early in the war and their uncanny secret weapons programs. Without Vril, the Germans would never have defeated their enemies in Poland, France, and—at least early in the war—Russia. There are even those who suggest that the Nazi movement reached its military peak because they found a way to tap into some Vril power and technology. Jet-powered weapons and missiles were developed and perfected by the Nazis long before Allied forces could get their hands on that technology. The notion of Vril also touches on something else that will be discussed in this book—foo fighters. Some people believe that the strange orbs that harassed and buzzed Allied fighter planes and bombers were not flying ships from another planet but secret weapons developed by German engineers or magicians, and fueled by Vril power.

Critics of the Vril power theory have one counter. Why did the Nazis lose?

Simple. Vril power—and all the other powers the Nazis tried to tap into—just wasn't as powerful as the magical forces that the Allies arrayed against Germany.

FORTEAN FORCES
IN WORLD WAR II

Charles Fort died in 1932, just as the winds of World War II began to kick up in the cities of Europe and the islands of the Pacific. Fort had spent a lifetime studying phenomena that drifted along the fringes of reality—everything from storms of frogs dropping from the sky to weird airships buzzing through the skies in the pre-aircraft era.

Even today, his books, including *Lo!* and *Book of the Damned*, are considered required reading by occultists and those interested in the supernatural. Fort's legacy is that he dared to study strange phenomena and explore the meaning behind it, rather than just write about it.

Had Fort lived to see World War II, there is no doubt that his list of anomalous phenomena would have grown exponentially. In this section, we will look at some of the events and activity that would have likely ended up in a Fortean list.

UFOs During World War II

World War II added another dimension to warfare—a third dimension. Although balloons and planes had been used in other conflicts, airpower came of age during World War II. Paranormally speaking, the action wasn't all on the ground either, and witnesses—who include well-trained pilots—suggest the phenomena they experienced during the war came not just from the third dimension, but from dimensions beyond ordinary time and space.

Fighter and bomber pilots who flew missions over Europe claimed that strange, glowing objects with unmatched speed and agility followed and harassed—and possibly even mounted attacks on—their formations. We will discuss these objects—which the pilots referred to as *foo fighters*, and you and I might label UFOs—in this section.

Not all the foo fighters were in Europe. In what's referred to as the Battle of Los Angeles, the West Coast of the United States may have witnessed the only battle between the armed to the teeth forces of humanity versus a craft—or crafts—piloted by extraterrestrial intelligence. If ETs came in peace during World War II, the antiaircraft gun-wielding welcoming committee may have made them leave in a hurry.

Foo Fighters

In late autumn of 1944, American pilots knitted into formations of bombers and fighters swarming the skies above Germany were always on high alert. Rogue German fighters could pounce on their planes the second they let their guard down, flak guns could blast metal shells their way at any moment. But the pilots were completely caught off guard by a new, mysterious presence that made itself known in the skies above Europe at the end of 1944.

The pilots and crews of these planes watched, mystified, as strange globs of light—often yellow or orange—shot into the air and darted through the sky. The objects often moved toward the formation. Thinking that enemy planes had them in their sights, pilots began evasive maneuvers and gunners stood by, ready for the inevitable conflict.

When the lights closed in, though, the crews were stunned that these craft did not look or move like any aircraft in the enemy's arsenal. They climbed at speeds beyond the acceleration of any aircraft at that time and darted through the formations in ways that would create g-forces strong enough to tear a human body apart.

Crews quickly dubbed the flying lights *foo fighters*, possibly after a comic strip catchphrase. They also used the less politically correct *kraut fireballs*. While current UFO theorists quickly jump to an extraterrestrial explanation, it's important to note that the Allied air`crews did not immediately entertain the idea that these objects were piloted by extraterrestrial crews. They believed they were facing a new German secret weapon. Throughout the war, in veiled messages and threats, Hitler insinuated that German scientists were about to unleash scores of secret weapons on the Allies. With V-2 rockets and jet planes scorching through the skies, the pilots were ready to believe that the foo fighters were a new phase in Germany's plan to win the war with secret weapons.

If they were, the weapons didn't seem to go on the attack. They seemed more interested in observing and toying with American bombers and fighters—not destroying them.

US Army Air Major William Leet reported on one such foo fighter encounter, according to Mack Maloney, a historian of wartime UFO sightings. In his book, *UFOs in Wartime: What They Didn't Want You to Know*, Maloney writes that Leet was piloting his B-17, called the Old Crow, over Austria in December of 1944. The plane was alone, taking part in a "lone wolf" mission, as he referred to it. Lone wolf missions were meant to surprise and frustrate the German air defense and air force crews who were used to massive Allied bombing raids with dozens of bombers.

Leet made visual contact with a strange object as he and his crew began to leave the airspace over Austria. He said the craft was a "perfectly" circular glowing amber light and estimated its size to be about ten feet in diameter. Oddly, he claimed that he had just looked at that piece of airspace seconds before and it was empty. A few seconds later, this light popped into view.

The pilot, with numerous missions and hundreds of hours of flying time under his belt, never saw the Germans fly anything like it and he definitely knew the Allied forces didn't have access to such a craft.

His crew was convinced that it was an attacking German aircraft and wanted to shoot at it, but Leet was convinced that, first, it wasn't a Nazi fighter and, second, because it wasn't demonstrating any form of hostile intentions, the strange object wasn't a threat at all. Leet commanded the crew to desist any hostile activity toward the craft.

Leet said that the craft remained peacefully content to fly with his B-17 for a long portion of the flight back to base. This gave him a long time to observe and study his strange escort. One thing he noticed was that the object didn't change—its speed, course, and luminosity were steady. This seemed to reinforce his initial observation that this was an intelligently controlled craft. A meteor would have changed size and shape, as well as quickly lose some of its shine going through the earth's atmosphere. A planet would have seemed to change direction as the plane changed course, but this object followed the bomber as it zeroed in on its home base.

Whether that intelligence was human or inhuman haunted Leet during the mission. He noticed a lack of exhaust. No man-made craft could have kept up that speed without producing some type of exhaust. Over time, Leet became convinced this was no German wonder weapon. It was something not of this world.

That idea was reinforced when the crew lost contact with their impromptu escort. Leet said it didn't bank or turn away. It didn't increase speed or change altitude. The object literally disappeared, just as suddenly as it had appeared.

When Leet and his crew landed, they reported the incident to the intelligence officer assigned to the squadron. The officer had a few suggestions for what the crew witnessed, but although the crew of the Old Crow never fired a shot at the object, they quickly and efficiently shot down all the theories that the intelligence officer floated their way. When the intelligence officer told Leet it was a German fighter, the pilot responded that the fighter never took hostile action against his crew. It would be kind of an odd strategy for a super-secret fighter plane not to take on a completely vulnerable bomber. When the officer guessed it was a spotter for German antiaircraft gunners, Leet said that during most of the mission, the plane was far from any antiaircraft batteries. That laid that theory to rest.

But no other squadron tangled with foo fighters quite like the pilots of the 415th Night Fighter Squadron, according to Maloney. Some experts suggest that these pilots were actually the ones to dub the strange crafts they witnessed *foo fighters*, although there's no way to tell for sure.

What makes their reports even more credible is that only special pilots could make it into the unit. Keen eyesight and outstanding skills of observation were needed. In other words, these are not the types of people who mistake the planet Venus for a hovering extraterrestrial mothership. They were also among the bravest pilots, in a force composed of brave pilots, to fly off in the night, completely vulnerable to German pilots and antiaircraft gunners.

On the night of November 26, 1944, those skills were put to the test in ways one veteran night fighter crew member of the 415th would have never imagined.

One crew jumped in their British-built Bristol Beaufighter, a multiseat fighter, and cruised out of the 415th's base in France, searching for German trains that might be delivering ammunition and supplies to troops. After destroying a few of those trains, the pilot noticed a red light appear and then track alongside his aircraft. The light came as close as about a half mile away from the plane before it disappeared. It didn't seem to be a big deal—the pilot mentioned the sighting in his debriefing session, but ended it there. The foo fighters, however, were not done with the 415th.

A veteran of the squadron—Lt. Donald Meiers—later reported that pilots encountered more than one group of foo fighters. He said there were red fireballs that would fly at the tips of the plane's wing, three balls of foo fighters appeared in a vertical row and flew in front of the planes, and another group of foo fighters—about fifteen of them— hovered in the distance. Some of the lights flickered on and off. With the Christmas holiday approaching, the pilot couldn't help but remark that the whole scene looked like a Christmas tree all decorated for the season.

Meiers, however, said at least one foo fighter was not in the Christmas spirit and chased his plane. He told a reporter that he was cruising down the Rhine Valley at about seven hundred feet when he noticed two strange fireballs—as he described them—flying with him. Not sure what they were and presuming a defensive posture, the pilot tried to out-maneuver the foo fighters. No such luck. He banked to the left. They tuned with him. He then banked right—and they immediately banked right.

"We were going 260 miles an hour and the balls were keeping right up with us," he said.

Some UFO historians say that radar operators—not pilots—may be the ones who initially called these odd aerial phenomena they witnessed *foo fighters*. While the debate on who gets credit for the nickname continues, radar operators at the time did receive odd returns on their scopes and saw strange activity on their screens. In some cases this phenomena coordinated with what pilots for the 415th were witnessing.

During the December incident, for example, radar operators saw blips on their screen that corresponded to the pilots' eyewitness encounters with foo fighters.

Another radar operator for an antiaircraft battalion, Andrew V. Armrose, reported that foo fighters were a somewhat common occurrence. Radar operators called these incidents "ghosts."

"I had frequently picked up a target on the radar screen that appeared to be a conventional aircraft," Armrose said. "But…upon being tracked [it] would accelerate to a fantastic speed, which made it impossible to set a rate on and even more difficult to identify. So we referred to them as 'ghosts'…I have always been puzzled by the occurrence of these sightings I have personally made on radar."

UFOs Over Normandy

It wasn't just pilots and crews of Allied aircraft that saw foo fighters. An American journalist who was reporting on the Normandy landing said he witnessed a strange craft in the sky above the invasion site, a craft that he struggled to identify, let alone explain.

According to George Todt, a reporter for the *Los Angeles Herald-Examiner*, he was on Omaha Beach one evening—the troops he was covering for the paper were about to break out of the beach and take on German forces in the interior of France. While walking on the beach, he looked up and noticed a "pulsating red fireball" in the sky, cruising overhead. He estimated the altitude of the aircraft or rocket, or whatever it was, to be about a half mile up.

The light—several times larger than any star in the sky that night—glided effortlessly overhead. Todt began to speculate—his first guess was that it was a new German weapon that the Allied forces called a *buzz bomb*. The rocket-powered V1s had started to fly out of German bases and into England just a few weeks before this sighting.

But there was a problem with that speculation and he knew it. This object was flying into German lines, not away from them. To hit England, the V-1s flew the exact opposite direction that this strange aircraft was flying.

Just the way the object maneuvered made the group of soldiers, including some high-ranking officers, arrive at the conclusion that it was definitely not a buzz bomb. The object moved over the beach and then halted directly above the German-American lines and hovered. It remained there for about seventeen minutes, Todt reported—and then flew away.

Maybe most of the witnesses to this Normandy incident had never heard the expression *foo fighters*. After all, it was a relatively new phenomenon. But they did realize they witnessed something strange and unexplainable that night, something most Fortean experts now place in the category of a World War II foo fighter.

Foo Fighters Over the Pacific

While most of the documented foo fighter engagements were reported by Allied crews over the battlefields of Europe, many pilots saw similar objects in the Pacific theater. According to the December 1945 issue of *VFW Magazine*, B-29 crews had several run-ins with crafts that closely matched what their colleagues were experiencing in Europe.

These fireballs followed the bombers so closely that some witnesses said the objects almost sat on the planes' tails. They changed colors rapidly, flashing from orange to red to white, and then repeating the cycle. With tales of devastating kamikaze attacks not far in the back of their minds, pilots initially thought the strange aircraft were these Japanese suicide pilots, but just as the sightings in Europe prompted no attacks, the foo fighters were strangely passive with the massive bombers on attack runs to Japan.

In one disturbing encounter, the foo fighter chased an American B-29—one of the superfortresses that was delivering punishing bomb loads to Japan—into a cloud bank. Visibility was near zero in the cloud and the pilot believed there would be no way that the strange aircraft could predict his evasive maneuvers. His plane would be nearly invisible. However, when he pulled his bomber out of the clouds, the foo fighter was right there, matching his twists and turns with impeccable precision. It was so close—about five hundred yards away—that the pilot could better describe the foo fighter. He reported that it was about three feet in diameter and was wrapped in a phosphorescent red and orange glow. He didn't notice any wings, tail, or rudder that would suggest a conventional airframe, either a plane or missile.

Just like in the encounters of other crews who claimed to have seen foo fighters, this object mysteriously disappeared. The crew of the B-29 said that as they approached the target—and as the sunlight began to appear—the foo fighter suddenly vanished.

The magazine reports on one more foo fighter sighting in the Pacific; a B-24 Liberator crew saw one as it cruised high above Truk Lagoon, a once formidable Japanese naval base in the Caroline Islands. According to this crew's report, they were flying about eleven thousand feet over Truk Lagoon when they noticed two red glowing balls of light rising into the air and heading toward them, closing in fast.

During the flight, the orbs kept in close contact with the Liberator. One twisted around and returned to base— or wherever the hell it came from—according to the crew. The other light stayed close to the plane though. Sometimes it was right beside the plane, sometimes slightly behind. Other times the light swung in front of the bomber, obviously not afraid that it would lose contact with the plane. Eventually, soon after daybreak, the light soared up a few thousand feet and went out of sight.

The bomber crew radioed a nearby radar installation to get an assessment of enemy aircraft in the area.

The response: There were no enemy planes in the area.

Secret Weapons or UFO Observers?

So, what were the foo fighters and why did they seem so keen to keep a close eye on Allied aircraft?

In 1944, the answer seemed to be unanimous: the aircraft were German weapons. They may have been remote-controlled machines, some speculated. German scientists and engineers had made great progress in building remote-controlled aircraft.

The lack of offensive capabilities seemed to cause doubt in many, though. Why build a remote-controlled airplane that just safely tags along with an Allied formation? There was also the matter of the performance of the crafts. Nearly all of the reports about foo fighters include details that are hard to explain through the performance of known aircraft of the time. The crafts are said to make instant stops and hover, attain great speeds, instantly disappear, and match the quick turns and dives of top-of-the-line fighter planes with ease.

Another theory is that the Nazis created foo fighters as a secret weapon and that the aim of the weapon was psychological. They were just remote-controlled planes designed to scare pilots, the theory goes. If true, no documents on such a project have turned up in exhaustive searching and cataloging of the Nazi military weapons, nor did Nazi officers reveal the existence of such a plan during equally exhaustive interrogations. One would think that after decades of searching the same files and hearing the same testimonies that revealed the most closely held secrets of the German war machine (like the V-2) that we would also uncover the foo fighter secret.

The military decided that foo fighters were natural phenomena—either ball lightning or St. Elmo's fire. The problem with both of those theories is that the phenomena in question are both rare and short-lived. It's doubtful, for instance, that ball lightning is going to tag along with a B-17 for forty minutes. They aren't known to create radar signatures, either.

Although the military wanted to pass the buck and suggest more natural explanations for foo fighters, an inconvenient fact confronted them: The quality of the observers who witnessed foo fighters and the exacting details of their observations pointed toward controlled flight, not natural phenomena. After all, there are no better observers of aerial phenomena than pilots. And there was no better time for trained observers than during World War II. These are pilots who could see a mere dot on the horizon and tell you the aircraft's make and model—and whether it was hostile. Their lives—and the lives of their crew—depended on such keen powers of observation. At no time in history were more pilots—trained observers—in the skies. Pilots during World War II also spent an unusual amount of time in the sky and witnessed a range of aerial phenomena, from meteorites to strange electromagnetic and weather-related phenomena. They knew the difference between a bolt of lightning or a streaking meteorite and an intelligently piloted craft, in other words.

In fact, as mentioned, in some cases the sightings lasted for a relatively long time. It defies the imagination that a pilot who could spot an enemy fighter and prepare a counter maneuver in a few seconds could not spot signs of a conventional aircraft or natural aerial phenomenon when they had observed the object for nearly an hour.

Although the debate rages, foo fighters remain one of World War II's most enduring aerial mysteries.

The Battle of Los Angeles

From late February 24 to the early morning of February 25, 1942, the city of Los Angeles was startled awake by explosive flashes and the sweeping beams of spotlights frantically scanning the sky. These weren't the popping flashbulbs and swinging spotlights of the latest movie premiere. This was war, and the city—apparently—was under attack.

Historians mostly blame the bizarre event now known as the Battle of Los Angeles or the Great Los Angeles Air Raid simply on a lethal combination of war jitters—Pearl Harbor happened just a few months before—mixed with mistaken identity. The event has since been satirized and ridiculed. Steven Spielberg directed the comedy *1941*, starring John Belushi and Dan Aykroyd, which was inspired by that night's events. The movie suggested that the people of LA may have let Hollywood's zeal for war movies cloud their judgment about actual war.

After the war, the Japanese revealed there were no air-craft—at least ones they dispatched—over LA that night. And war records seem to corroborate that Spielberg's version of the air raid was much closer to reality.

But there's another side to this. Many witnesses, while discounting a Japanese attack or any type of conventional enemy aircraft in the air, still believe there actually was something in the sky that night. These are credible and sober witnesses, too. They don't seem to be the type of people who would be swept up in *war jitters*, as the War Department called it. And they say the object they saw was far more disconcerting than even a fleet of marauding enemy aircraft.

The late C. Scott Littleton, a professor of anthropology at Occidental College in Los Angeles, was one of those witnesses and, although not a ufologist, believed what he saw that night was something more than a stray blimp or misidentified warplanes.

According to his account, he was just a child living with his parents and extended family in a home near Hermosa Beach, California, when the blasts of antiaircraft fire woke him. He looked out the window and could see the flashes of antiaircraft gunfire and the frantic scanning of searchlight beams. Initially, he said the activity didn't scare him. Gunners routinely practiced on targets towed behind aircraft. But something about the ferocity of the barrage and the confusion of the searchlights, as well as the timing—most of the night exercises were earlier in the evening so that residents' sleep wouldn't be disturbed—caused Littleton concern. And soon enough the rest of his family began to feel the same way.

His father, a neighborhood air raid warden, had received no alerts about a drill, and frantically tried to contact the authorities, while huddling his family together and ordering them into the makeshift bomb shelter in the basement. Littleton remembered listening to the sharp report of the guns raking the skies while he and his mother, along with his grandparents, talked nervously.

It was Littleton's mother who took the first brave step to investigate. She walked out of their makeshift bunker and headed toward the beach. Littleton followed, half afraid that his mother would tell him to return to the basement. Shrapnel was falling on the beach and there was a roar of planes overhead, which Littleton thought might be the enemy aircraft. He discovered they were pursuit planes later, but that was before he saw what the planes were pursuing.

Looking out on the Pacific Ocean, Littleton and his mother gasped as they saw an object floating about the sea. The spotlights zeroed right in on a silvery "lozenge-shaped bug" hanging in the night sky. There was no moon that night, so there was no mistaking the object for a celestial body.

The one thing that the witnesses immediately noticed was that the object stood nearly motionless. It hovered completely still, and they estimated that it hung between four thousand and eight thousand feet above the ocean. That ability to hover without making a sound was unlike anything Littleton had ever seen among the numerous military aircraft that practiced in the area.

The gunners were obviously looking at the same object. The explosions from the antiaircraft shells concentrated on the silver object floating above the sea. Streams of spotlights had the object in their sights as well. In fact, one famous photo shows the craft surreally poised in the crosshairs of several spotlight beams.

Meanwhile, shrapnel from these shots began to rain down on the mother and son, who backed up to the house so the falling debris would not hit them.

Littleton noticed one odd thing: despite the gunfire, the craft took neither defensive action to get out of harm's way or aggressive action against the gunners. Both seemed to be in its capabilities, according to Littleton. None of the rounds that appeared to land near or on the craft had any effect.

After taking a brutal fusillade from everything the American military could throw at it, the ship began to drift unscathed toward Redondo Beach.

The family noticed some other strange activity that night. Right after the UFO disappeared and the gunfire ceased, they heard aircraft engines roaring overhead. They seemed to be following the craft. Littleton guessed that the engine sounds were P-38s from a nearby airfield, and he believed they were called out to give chase to the bizarre craft they just witnessed.

Other witnesses confirmed the Littleton's encounter. An artist and interior decorator identified only as "Katie" volunteered as an air raid warden for west LA. She was sleeping in the early morning hours of February 25 when her air raid supervisor called and told her to be on the lookout for a plane flying very near her home. Katie went to the nearest window and looked out. She saw exactly what her supervisor had described, but it didn't look like anything described in an enemy aircraft identification chart.

"It was huge," she said. "It was just enormous."

During the air raid, authorities issued an order to turn out the lights, which had an unforeseen effect, an effect that UFO hunters in urban areas hardly ever experience. Los Angeles—the city of bright lights—became deathly dark, offering unmatched vistas of the sky and stars. In the uncluttered sky, Katie could make out details of the craft perfectly.

"It was a lovely pale orange and about the most beautiful thing you've ever seen. I could see it perfectly because it was very close," she reported. "It was big!"

Katie saw the searchlight beams zero in on the craft, which hovered in one spot for a long time, just as the Littletons described. She, too, saw other aircraft in the area, but noticed they turned around shortly before the barrage of antiaircraft guns opened fire on the object.

The next morning, those charged with the defense of Los Angeles issued a hastily written report of the incident. It was not the Japanese, the report said, and, if you read between the lines, it was definitely not a spacecraft from another planet. The defense officials blamed the incident, at various times, on normal war jitters, a balloon, and weather conditions. However, most eyewitnesses did not buy the official line and it remains one of World War II's most hotly debated incidents.

The Philadelphia Experiment

If there actually was a Philadelphia Experiment, Fortean researchers believe it was an experiment to see how far reality—and perhaps the truth—can be twisted and transformed.

The story—and there are considerable variations—goes a little like this:

The USS *Eldridge*, a *Cannon*-class destroyer escort launched on July 25, 1943, was docked in the Philadelphia Naval Yard. Sometime after its launch and before its commissioning, rumors swirled that technicians were outfitting the ship with advanced technology. Some sailors believed it was a new radar system, while others heard that the equipment had something to do with not just new technology, but new physics. Other rumors claimed Albert Einstein and quantum physicists were involved. The physicists were basing the technology on a "unified field theory," a theory that would unite the small world of quantum physics with the huge world of swirling galaxies and the universe itself. And, oh yeah, the technology could bend time and space itself. The military was interested in the theory because they believed they could make warships invisible. The navy believed this cloaking device would make their ships nearly impervious to attack from enemy boats and planes.

Other theories suggest that the work of the famous Serbian scientist Nikola Tesla guided the experiment and that its true goal was to master gravity.

According to the stories, a few small experiments were successfully carried out. Those reports said the ship nearly disappeared, leaving a greenish fog lingering in the harbor momentarily. There were some troubling warning signs, however. Sailors on board the ship said they felt sick after the experiment.

Other experiments were scheduled and the equipment was quickly reset. Then things took an unexpectedly scary turn, according to several experts including Charles Berlitz, who wrote *The Philadelphia Experiment*, the seminal work on the case.

In one account, the equipment either was not calibrated at all or not calibrated correctly, and the ship completely disappeared during an experiment.

But it didn't simply vanish. Somehow, it was teleported. According to some reports, witnesses said they saw a brilliant blue flash and the massive USS *Eldridge* was gone.

About two hundred miles away, sailors steaming through the Atlantic aboard a merchant marine ship, the SS *Andrew Furuseth*, were stunned to see the ship appear instantly before them. They watched the destroyer for a few minutes and then—as quickly as it appeared—it was gone. Vanished.

Back in Philadelphia, the stunned experimenters stared at the empty spot in the ocean that the Eldridge had occupied only seconds ago. They waited for ten minutes, according to some sources. Each moment passed by more painful than the last. And then it reappeared.

Whether or not the experiment was a success depends on the source, however. More disturbing reports suggest the injuries were horrific, going far beyond the nausea experienced by a few sailors. There are stories that men were "melted" into metal equipment. Their arms and legs welded into the floor and walls of the ship. Deaths were reported.

Those who believe in the Philadelphia Experiment offer the explanation that the gruesome injuries and deaths may be tied to why the experiments—which were, on the surface, successful—were quickly halted and the results made top secret. They also suggest that intelligence officials did not want this new powerful technology, which they obviously couldn't control, to fall into enemy hands.

The experiment remained completely secret.

Then, years later, in 1955, the story began to leak out. It started when astronomer and researcher Morris K. Jessup received a strange reply from a reader of his book. A copy of Jessup's book, *The Case for the UFO*, with strange annotations, was mailed to the Office of Naval Research, which then contacted Jessup. Jessup's book explored theories that could explain the propulsion of flying saucers that were the focus of hundreds of headlines in the United States.

From what Jessup could decipher, the annotations were from someone who was familiar with an experiment that had tested some of Jessup's theories on propulsion—from antigravity to electromagnetic manipulation. The marked-up copy of Jessup's book, along with a string of letters from a writer, revealed a person who was poised perilously between being fascinating and insane. This man would be known forever in Fortean history as Carlos Allende (or Carl Allen), the man who broke the news—or spun the tale—about the Philadelphia Experiment. In those letters, Allende said that he witnessed at least one bizarre outcome of the Philadelphia Experiment—he was one of the crew members on board the SS *Andrew Furuseth* when the *Eldridge* appeared out of nowhere.

Allende's subsequent stories seemed unbelievable to Jessup, but he found that if the man's story was made up he was a brilliant hoaxer. Allende included his sailor identification information that confirmed he was on board the *Andrew Furuseth* at the time of the incident. It wasn't just Jessup who wanted to meet the mysterious seaman; the navy was interested too. Allende proved to be difficult quarry, even for these naval intelligence experts. Over time, his story became mixed with folklore and fakelore from hoaxers. He later resurfaced with more information and contacted UFO experts, but those disclosures only muddied the already murky story of the *Eldridge*.

Skeptics stepped up with a possible explanation. They said that, indeed, the Philadelphia Experiment was a test of invisibility, but it was a test to make the ship invisible to enemy torpedoes, not to teleport the ship back in time and melt people to the decks. In fact, there was no equipment or power source among the experimental equipment on board the ship that could perform such a feat. Instead, the electromagnetic technology was simply meant to confuse the torpedoes and make them miss their mark. Hence, the ship would be invisible, at least to torpedoes.

But, like a bizarre form of the telephone game, as rumors of the experiment passed from sailor to sailor on board the ship and through the base, tales about the experiment became more bizarre and more elaborate. Eventually a rumor became established that the scientists intended to make the ship completely invisible, not just to torpedoes. Propelled by Allende's testimony, the Philadelphia Experiment became one of World War II's most intriguing conspiracies, one that continues to be debated among both camps—believers and skeptics—even today.

World War II Coincidences and Curses

Ghosts on battleships, spirits sulking in trenches, and dozens of other manifestations of the paranormal make World War II truly weird, but there's another strange aspect to this global conflict.

Historians and paranormal theorists also list the many bizarre, almost unbelievable coincidences and stories of deadly curses as proof of World War II's haunted legacy. In the pages ahead, we will review some of those coincidences and synchronicities, ones that could have tipped off the Germans to the world's largest amphibious invasion and possible secret codes for a sneak attack. We'll also explore curses that may have kicked off a violent invasion.

The Curse of Tamerlane

It was a warm night in the Uzbekistan city of Samarkand. A group of Soviet scientists and archaeologists huddled outside a mound of earth they had dug on their quest to find the tomb of one of history's greatest leaders and most powerful military minds. Another group of writers, photographers, and cinematographers were nearby. They were called to be part of the expedition and document the historic excavation.

From what the writers were told, the scientists were about to open the tomb of Timur, better known in the Western world as Tamerlane.

Conqueror to his allies, butcher to his enemies, Timur was a Turkish-Mongolian chief who waged war across most of Asia and became the absolute most important ruler of his time when he defeated the Mamluks in Egypt and Syria. When Timur died in 1405, the ruler's ability to control the people of Eurasia did not diminish; it continued in a supernatural sense. After the final stone sealed Timur's tomb and the last shovel of dirt was dumped into place, folklorists say the construction team added one final piece to his everlasting memorial—a curse. The curse, these folklorists say, was simple: You open up the tomb and you will unleash a horde of hell on the world.

The Russian research team stood in front of the last obstacle that would lead them to what most of them pridefully declared the greatest archaeological find since the opening of King Tutankhamun's tomb in 1923. On June 19, 1941, the team rolled the stone from the burial vault and entered the warrior's burial chamber. The next day, they removed the large jade stone that rested on top of Tamerlane's grave itself. Instantly, the tomb filled with an acrid scent. The scientists coughed and gagged.

As men of science, the researchers found a natural reason for the smell. The ingredients of embalming fluid—resins, rose, and frankincense, most likely—caused the foul smell. After all, Tamerlane had died on a journey to China. To prepare for his burial back in Samarkand, he would have been embalmed. And the team had read the story of the smells that arose during the excavation of Tut's tomb. However, the researchers were forced to admit that the team that discovered Tut's remains said the scent was sweet, not grossly acrid.

Quickly dispelling any notion that something supernatural was behind the gut-wrenching smell, the researchers went about the excavation and—at least according to some reports—began removing Tamerlane's body for shipment back to Moscow.

The town of Samarkand buzzed. Hearing reports that the tomb was opened and that a strange scent issued from the body, the citizens in Samarkand shivered. They believed the smell was a sign that the curse that protected the king's tomb was set loose on the world. Taking Tamerlane's body from the grave defiled it even more. Believers cringed at what might happen next.

They didn't have to wait long to find out.

Two days after the opening of the tomb, another horde tore through Russia. This one, though, wasn't on horseback and armed with bows and arrows. This one was propelled into the Motherland on the steel treads of panzers and in the cockpits of screaming Stuka dive bombers.

Breaking a non-aggression pact with the Soviet Union, Nazi troops invaded the country. Not fools, the people of Samarkand recognized the similarity between Hitler and his hordes of Nazi troops and Tamerlane and his hordes of Turco-Mongol troops rampaging across Central Asia.

The legend goes one step further. The opening of the tomb may have unleashed the Tamerlane curse and caused World War II, but breaking the curse may have also led to the ultimate downfall of the Nazis' invasion of Russia. Believers in the legend said that news of the curse eventually reached Soviet leader Joseph Stalin. Maybe he believed in the curse, or maybe he just figured, after watching how the Nazis had steamrolled his best troops, that he couldn't take a chance. Stalin allegedly ordered Tamerlane's remains to be returned to Samarkand and interred with full honors.

A month after this, the Soviets won the battle of Stalingrad and the wave of Nazi domination began to recede.

Skeptics will point out that the Soviets beat back the Germans with superior manpower and technology. But they'll have a hard time convincing the people of Samarkand, who still believe that the curse—and the lifting of the curse—were too well-timed to be mere coincidence.

Precognitive Codes—
Did Messages Predict World War II Actions?

Strange signs in the skies are one thing, but Fortean phenomena in newspaper ads and crossword puzzles? It's true, according to Fortean experts. During the war, several bizarre coincidences were revealed that appeared to predict secret actions and plans that only the highest war planners knew.

These synchronicities unnerved the brass so much that they launched investigations, which turned up nothing.

They were just coincidences. But read on and decide for yourself: are these incidents just the result of random chance, or is there some force behind it? Maybe not an Allied force or an Axis force, but a Fortean force.

The D-Day Synchronicities

The Allied invasion of Europe was one of the most closely guarded secrets of the war, if not in all of history. A cadre of intelligence and counterintelligence officers created elaborate plans to hide the true objectives of the invasion, including landing sites, code words, and timelines. An entire dummy army, complete with fake radio traffic, inflatable armor, and loudspeakers blaring recorded sounds of military life, was created to bluff possible German spies into believing that the invasion would be at Calais, not Normandy.

All of these precautions and ruses were created with a real fear that if German intelligence officers discovered even small pieces of the invasion plan, they could determine the time and place of the attack and alert German military officials, who would then wait for the Allied invaders to hit the beach and pounce on them, sending the soldiers to the grave or back across the sea.

Early reports said that the intelligence work was achieving its goals. The Nazis did not seem to be shifting forces or making plans to counteract the invasion of Normandy.

And then a few officers from the elite British counter-espionage agency, MI5, started to work on the crossword puzzle of the British paper, *The Daily Telegraph*. They noticed that several clues and answers were related to the pending invasion, and some were even actual code words.

On May 2, 1944, the crossword puzzle clues included this one: "One of the U.S." The answer was the four-letter word, *Utah*. It turns out that was the code name for the beach—Utah Beach—that the US 4th Infantry Division was slated to storm on June 6. At the end of the month, the crossword contained this clue: "Red Indian on the Missouri." The answer, of course, was *Omaha*, which was also the code name for another beach the Americans were expected to hit.

As D-Day drew closer, intelligence officers were startled as the invasion-related clues began to appear in the crossword at an unprecedented rate, a rate that was simply outside of the realm of coincidence. On May 27, the actual code name for the invasion itself—*Overlord*—appeared. On May 30, the word *mulberry* was the solution to a clue. Mulberry was the name for an artificial harbor that would be constructed after the invasion to help the Allies move supplies and weapons into the heart of France.

On June 1, *Neptune*, a code name for the naval part of the initial attack, was used in the puzzle. If the MI5 agents looked back further in the crossword puzzle's history, they would have noticed other clues had been used. *Gold* and *sword* were solutions to clues a few months earlier. Those two were also code names for beaches where Canadian forces were supposed to land.

The MI5 agents went into action. They marched into the *Telegraph's* office and found Leonard Dawe, the man who created the paper's popular puzzles. Dawe was completely taken aback by the agents' insinuations and their interrogation, which was pretty thorough.

He was later quoted in a *Telegraph* article as saying, "They turned me inside out. They went to Bury St Edmunds where my senior colleague Melville Jones (the paper's other crossword compiler) was living and put him through the works. But they eventually decided not to shoot us after all."

The MI5 agents were—probably for once in their careers—baffled. They couldn't figure out how all the code words became public. The idea that coincidence could explain all of the code words tested even the most open-minded agents on the counterintelligence team. Still, with no real proof, they decided coincidence was the only real culprit.

Since the war, historians and experts on the paranormal who try to explain the D-Day crossword coincidences have split into two camps. Some historians choose a rational explanation. Dawe wasn't just a crossword puzzle master; he was also the headmaster at the Strand School. According to former students, Dawe often allowed them to come up with crossword clues. These sources suggest that students there often came in contact with Allied soldiers. They believe that these soldiers unwittingly discussed some of the codes and objectives, and that the students passed these on as cross-word clues when they helped Dawe.

For those familiar with the supernatural, the sheer number of code words makes the explanation that students passed on the codes unlikely. Would the soldiers accidentally pass on one or two code words to students? Possibly. But five or six? This would require several steps. The soldiers would need access to the code words—and they were still secret. Knowing that their lives and the lives of their comrades may be at risk, the soldiers would need frequent contact with the students, enough to trust them with the codes. And the students would need to be brazen enough to jeopardize the D-Day operation by inserting the clues into the puzzles.

Paranormal theorists have another explanation. They suggest that in periods of intense emotions, like war or pending battles, the powers of thought transference—telepathy—increase for both the sender and the receiver. The hypothesis is partially backed up theoretically by philosophers and psychologists such as Carl Jung, who said that people could deposit thoughts and ideas, as well as tap into other ideas and thoughts that lie in a collective unconscious. It's probably aptly described as a collective unconscious because there's very little conscious manipulation of such a field. It seems to operate in much deeper levels of being, if it exists at all.

In the case of the D-Day invasion, the soldiers who knew the codes transmitted them unconsciously into this field and the puzzle makers pulled them out and used them in their crosswords.

The sides supporting each explanation of the D-Day synchronicities are still deeply divided to this day.

Pearl Harbor Prediction:
Coded Message or Creepy Coincidence?

The readers of the *New Yorker* got more than the great writing and somewhat funny comics that the magazine was famous for when they opened their magazine on November 22, 1941. A series of ads scattered throughout the magazine would go down in infamy, either as a bizarre coincidence, an eerie prediction, or a diabolical coded message to enemies preparing for the attack on Pearl Harbor.

A few weeks before bombs rained down on American soil, the peculiar advertisements contained an ominous—and prescient—bit of copywriting. One ad read: "Achtung, Warning, Alerte! We hope you'll never have to spend a long winter's night in an air-raid shelter, but we were just thinking ... it's only common sense to be prepared. If you're not too busy between now and Christmas, why not sit down and plan a list of the things you'll want to have on hand ... And though it's no time, really, to be thinking of what's fashionable, we bet that most of your friends will remember to include those intriguing dice and chips which make Chicago's favorite game The Deadly Double."

The smaller ads were even more intriguing, if not so ominous. These small blocks featured drawings of dice with the numbers twelve and seven prominently displayed on the die and facing toward the reader. The copy referred the reader back to the main ad.

Rumor has it that intelligence officers never noticed the obscure ad before the attack on Pearl Harbor, but it came to their attention soon after. According to the story, they sent an investigator to the offices of the *New Yorker* to find out who placed the ad, but it was strictly a cash deal. There was no name, and the investigation died.

Scattered throughout the issue were six smaller ads referring back to the main copy, with the dice numbered twelve and seven, numbers on no known dice. Later during the war, navy transport pilot Joseph Bell was flying a South Pacific route when one of his passengers, an intelligence officer, told him that many in intelligence considered this ad a secret warning. He had been assigned to investigate the matter, but every lead had led to a dead end—the ad's copy had been presented in person at the magazine's offices, and the fee paid with cash. Neither the game offered in the ad, nor the company that purported to make it, ever existed.

The intelligence officers were convinced that the ad was nothing more than a coded message to other Japanese intelligence operators in the country of a pending attack. Perhaps it was a way to warn them the attack was imminent and they should prepare to flee the country.

After the war, though, the wife of the man who placed the ads supposedly stepped forward and claimed the weird copy was not a coded message to Japanese agents; rather, it was trying to drum up interest in a board game that the man was trying to sell nationwide. The copy's references to bombings and the ominous dice with the numbers twelve and seven staring out at the reader were nothing more than coincidence.

While paranormal theorists have no trouble believing that the advertiser was not an agent of the Japanese military, they do believe the man may have been an agent of a much deeper, more pervasive force—the power of synchronicity. Based on Jung's theories, synchronicity is an acausal connection between events, which is often called coincidence. However, the perceiver recognizes a deep meaning between the events. It's more meaningful than the quirky but random events that we typically call coincidence.

For instance, clocks stopping at the exact time a loved one passes away or when you're looking at a person's picture on your phone and they call you. According to Jung, we are all connected to a much larger form of consciousness—something he called the collective unconscious—that often reveals itself in unpredictable ways and often uses symbols to transmit its messages. Certainly, Jungians would see the dice—the ultimate symbol of fate—as a message that could suggest something like an imminent attack that would dramatically change the course of the country's history. This *overmind*, as some other philosophers refer to the collective unconscious, sits outside of space and time. It can reveal hidden things of the past—ghosts might be an example of this—and offer glimpses, albeit veiled glimpses, into the future.

For people who favor the paranormal explanation, the Pearl Harbor synchronicities are an indication that this marketer had tapped into this field. He connected two things: advertisements for his game and the premonition of the future attack. Or, perhaps more accurately, he served unconsciously as the medium for the synchronistic connection. He, of course, had no idea that the symbols he used—the twelve and the seven, along with the violent warlike imagery—were a deeper message, a warning.

That the message went unheeded is perhaps not the point. The mystery of synchronicity is that it is not to warn someone to change their actions, it's to alert them to the presence of a deep connection between them and the universe, some Jungian experts suggest.

If that's the case, the mission of the Pearl Harbor synchronicity—which has intrigued World War II history buffs and paranormal enthusiasts alike—was accomplished.

CONCLUSION: HAUNTS, HEROES, AND HALLOWED REMINDERS

"There is no proof nor yet any denial. We were, we are, and we will be." —General George Patton in a letter to his mother, 1917

We've had a chance to scan the skies for ghost planes flying over the United Kingdom. We've landed on haunted beaches that were once stormed, decades ago, by thousands of soldiers. We've probed the battlefields of Europe for ghosts and spirits connected to the violent action of World War II. In the Pacific and Atlantic Oceans, we found evidence of paranormal activity on board World War II battleships and aircraft carriers. Tales of signs and synchronicities during the war also seem to suggest that other forces—occult forces—drove the fate of the war almost as much as the armed forces engaged in the conflict.

So, did this reconnaissance mission into haunted World War II make you a believer in ghosts and the supernatural?

Before you answer that question, let me chime in. I've written a bunch of books about ghosts, covering everything from the spirits of dead rock stars to haunted universities. What I've found is that behind these fun, weird, and creepy tales are layers of folklore, mythology, psychology, sociology, and even fringe science. Broadly speaking, the paranormal encounters in this volume and my other books come in two shades: ghostlore, and what I tend to refer to as ghost accounts.

Ghostlore, as its name suggests, is simply folklore that incorporates ghosts and spirits. How ghostlore arises and circulates is nearly as mysterious as the appearance of an apparition. Until the advent of the internet, ghostlore was mainly an oral tradition. People spread ghostlore by word of mouth, the tales often growing creepier and spookier with each retelling. Details often changed, giving rise to dozens of variations. Each generation subtly alters these tales as well. These stories are rarely told in the first person and it's almost impossible to nail down an original source. I would say that most of the ghost stories we are all familiar with would be placed in this category.

Not all ghost stories can be dispatched as mere folklore, however. I place first-person stories involving purported paranormal activity into the ghost accounts category. But you can't automatically jump to the conclusion that these accounts, even ones from reliable witnesses, are actually supernatural. They could be the result of hallucinations or optical illusions, for example. Others could be the result of misinterpreted natural phenomena. The clawing of a ghostly hand against the wall may just be the gnawing teeth of a rodent who became trapped between rooms. The ghastly closing of a door late at night might be a gust of wind blown through the walls of a drafty home. Finally, intentional deception can't be ruled out for some of the accounts either.

But still, a portion of first-person accounts withstands these skeptical probes. The accounts come from reliable witnesses not prone to hallucinations and from people who first try very hard to debunk the activity they encountered, in order to rule out natural phenomena. Some witnesses are trained observers. While first-person ghost accounts represent a minority of the collected legacy of haunted World War II, these witnesses and their stories do exist.

And while I'm at it, I should also point out that it is possible that some of the stories I tend to brush off as fictional ghostlore may have been initiated by people who really did have an encounter with something that they couldn't explain. Someone who wished to remain anonymous may have told the story of their specific encounter, which could then become embedded in a larger tapestry of haunted legends. In other words, those original sources were lost, leaving just echoes of their spooky encounters.

Still not convinced?

That's okay. As a former journalist who tries to practice open-minded skepticism, I also rapidly and perpetually vacillate between believer and non-believer. But before you decide that these war ghost stories are—like General Anthony Clement McAuliffe's assessment of the German demand for his troops' surrender during the Battle of the Bulge—"nuts," and before you think that maybe the last few hundred pages of material you read were a complete waste of time, I want you to consider one thing. Even if every detail and every account in *Haunted World War II* belongs in the fiction and fantasy category, there still may be good reasons to read—and even study—ghost stories.

First, these ghost stories tend to serve as oral and written memorials for the heroes of World War II. Think of it as non-living history. It's nearly impossible to tell a ghost story or listen to a ghost story without revealing real information about the characters and events covered in the story. Ghost stories in this book, for example, introduced us to important historical concepts like the invasion of Normandy and the Eastern Front, and important historical figures—Winston Churchill and Abraham Lincoln's ghost or Ike in his Gettysburg farmhouse, for instance. With each telling of these World War II ghost stories and tales of occult weirdness, we introduce a new generation or a new student to details about this important time in world history.

Second, throughout literary history, ghost stories are also told as cautionary tales that help point the way to good behavior and steer us away from actions that might harm us or our loved ones. The ghosts who populated William Shakespeare's works and the squad of spirits in Charles Dickens's *A Christmas Carol* are good examples of these mystical mentors. Could these ghosts of World War II, then, exist as permanent reminders of the horrors of war and the senseless loss of human life during the atrocities that darken that bloody era of world history?

To sum it up, I hope that the previous chapters have not just entertained you, but given you something to think about. In the words of paranormal investigator and writer Jeff Belanger, "History is a ghost story." And, if this is so, maybe we should especially pay attention to ghost stories that arise during eras of tremendous conflict, because these would undoubtedly produce the most important—and most terrifying—history lessons possible.

NOTES AND BIBLIOGRAPHY

Chapter 1

"21 People Describe Their Encounters With The Paranormal And The Stories Will Give You Nightmares." Thought Catalog. April 4, 2014. http://thoughtcatalog.com/hok-leahcim/2014/04/21-people-describe-their-encounters-with-the-paranormal-and-the-stories-will-give-you-nightmares/.

Crain, Mary Beth. *Haunted U.S. Battlefields: Ghosts, Hauntings, and Eerie Events from America's Fields of Honor.* Guilford: Globe Pequot Press, 2008.

Gaddis, Vincent H. "Phantom Armies Out of Time."
Journal of Borderland Research 46, no. 6 (November &
December 1990): 14-18. https://borderlandsciences.org
/journal/vol/46/n06/Gaddis_on_Phantom_Armies.html.

"Ghost stories from WW2." Axis History Forum. Accessed
December 16, 2016. http://forum.axishistory.com
/viewtopic.php?t=75365.

"Ghostly stories, unexplained phenomena spook Pacific
troops." Okinawa Stripes, October 24, 2012.
http://okinawa.stripes.com/travel./ghostly-stories
-unexplained-phenomena-spook
-pacific-troops#sthash.aFaSa401.dpbs.

"Haunted Tunnel." Corregidor Forum. Accessed October
17, 2016. http://corregidor.proboards.com/thread/401
/haunted-tunnel.

Hitchcock, Jayne A. *The Ghosts of Okinawa*. York: Shiba
Hill, 2010.

"Japanese Ghosts Haunt Corregidor." Japan Probe.
Accessed October 17, 2016. http://www.japanprobe
.com/2006/06/12/japanese-ghosts-haunt-corregidor/.

Jayne Hitchcock (blog). Accessed August 9, 2016.
http://www.jahitchcock.com/.

KingAddison. "Normandy, Omaha beach Ghost?"
Reddit Paranormal Forum. 2014. https://www
.reddit.com/r/Paranormal/comments/1w9bgt
/normandy_omaha_beach_ghost/.

"Military spots where spirts are said to roam." *Military Times*, October 27, 2013. http://www.militarytimes .com/story/military/archives/2013/10/27/military -spots-where-spirits-are-said-to-roam/78543056/.

"Okinawa Spooky Sites Tour." *Nothing but Room* (blog). October 26, 2012. http://nothingbutroomblog .com/2012/10/okinawa-spooky-sites-tour.html.

Rogers, Thomas. "The Nazi Ghosthunters." *Pacific Standard*, October 5, 2015. https://psmag.com /social-justice/the-nazi-ghosthunters.

Shimoyachi, Nao. "War dead said to haunt Iwojima." *Japan Times*, October 22, 2003. http://www.japantimes.co.jp /news/2003/10/22/national/war-dead-said-to-haunt -iwojima/#.WKGDVW8rKM8.

Sudakov, Dmitry. "Tomb Raiders Digging WWII Graves Witness Inexplicable Phenomena." Pravda. October 30, 2009. http://www.pravdareport.com/science /mysteries/30-10-2009/110207-tomb_raiders-0/.

The Day Brothers. "Point du Hoc, Normandy." Ghosts and Stories. Accessed October 13, 2017. http://ghostsandstories.com/point-du-hoc -normandy.html.

"The Man in the Attic." Your Ghost Stories. May 12, 2015. http://www.yourghoststories.com/real-ghost-story .php?story=21786.

Walsh, Michael. "The Ghosts of the Eastern Front."
   Spingola.com. Accessed October 15, 2017.
   http://www.spingola.com/MW/ghosts.html.

Notes:
- Information about ghost stories in Europe also
  gathered during an email interview exchange
  with German-based paranormal researcher Tom
  Pedall, in addition to the group's Facebook page,
  Ghosthunter NRWUP.

Chapter 2

Arnold, Neil. *Shadows in the Sky: The Haunted Airways of
   Britain*. Stroud, UK: The History Press, 2012.

"Couple tell of 'ghost' plane mystery."
   Craven Herald & Pioneer. January 23, 2004.
   http://www.cravenherald.co.uk/news/8005534
   .Couple_tell_of__ghost__plane_mystery/.

French, Katie. "Walking with shadows! Eerie footage
   captures the moment the 'ghost of an RAF pilot' passes
   within inches of a father visiting an abandoned air
   base." Daily Mail. March 23, 2017. http://www
   .dailymail.co.uk/news/article-4341658/Footage
   -captures-ghost-RAF-pilot.html#ixzz4c.

"Ghost Plane!" *Angels and Ghosts* (blog). Accessed October
   19, 2017. http://www.angelsghosts.com/ghost_plane.

"Ghosts of Hickham." Your Ghost Stories. June 27, 2012. http://www.yourghoststories.com/real-ghost-story.php?story=15710.

Haining, Peter. *The Mammoth Book of True Hauntings*. London: Constable & Robinson, 2008.

Haskew, Michael E. "American Aviators Aloft at Pearl Harbor." HistoryNet. Accessed December 7, 2017. http://www.historynet.com/american-aviators-aloft-pearl-harbor.htm.

Jack. "WHAT?!! 'Phantom Ghost Fortress' B-17 That Landed at an Airfield—NO Crew Were on Board!!" War History Online. September 11, 2015. https://www.warhistoryonline.com/world-war-ii/what-phantom-ghost-fortress-b-17-that-landed-at-an-airfield-no-crew-were-on-board.html.

Kristen. "The Ghost of Hickam AFB." Castle of Spirits. Accessed October 20, 2017. https://web.archive.org/web/20160819200622/http://www.castleofspirits.com/stories05/hickham.html.

Lennon, Jen. "The Creepiest Ghost Stories and Legends from WWII." Ranker. Accessed October 19, 2017. http://www.ranker.com/list/creepy-ww2-ghost-stories/jenniferlennon.

Mills, Eric. *The Spectral Tide: True Ghost Stories of the U.S. Navy*. Annapolis: Naval Institute Press, 2009.

Powell, Jennette. "My Town Monday: Haunted Aircraft at the USAF Museum." *Jennette Marie Powell* (blog). October 31, 2011. http://jenpowell.com/blog /mtm-haunted-aircraft/.

Seaburn, Paul. "Ghost Plane Seen by Multiple Witnesses in England." Mysterious Universe. August 14, 2015. http://mysteriousuniverse.org/2015/08 /ghost-plane-seen-by-multiple-witnesses-in-england/.

Severn, Joey. "More witnesses to mystery 'ghost plane' over Derbyshire come forward." *The Derby Telegraph*. Removed from site and archived here: http://web .archive.org/web/20151015034232/http://www .derbytelegraph.co.uk:80/witnesses-mystery-flight -come-forward/story-27574679-detail/story.html.

Swancer, Brett. "The Spectral WWII Bombers of the United Kingdom." Mysterious Universe. Archived here: http://webcache.googleusercontent.com/search?q=cache :P4G8uhq6FNkJ:mysteriousuniverse.org/2015/07/the -spectral-wwii-bombers-of-the-united-kingdom/+&cd =3&hl=en&ct=clnk&gl=us.

"Tales From The Base: Schofield Barracks And AMR... Story #6." *Army Wife 101* (blog). October 24, 2014. http://armywife101.com/2014/10/tales-base -schofield-barracks-amr-story-6.html.

"The aeronautical hall of Halloween horrors."
Playbuzz. October 28, 2015. http://www
.playbuzz.com/sierrahotelaeronautics10
/the-aeronautical-hall-of-halloween-horrors.

"The Air Force Museum" page and comments. Real
Haunts. Accessed October 20, 2017. http://www
.realhaunts.com/united-states/the-air-force-museum/.

The Sun. "The mysterious UK 'ghost plane' that's been
spotted for decades." *New York Post*, February 14, 2017.
http://nypost.com/2017/02/14/the-mysterious-uk
-ghost-plane-thats-been-spotted-for-decades/.

"The Haunting of RF398." Office 23. Accessed October
10, 2017. https://office23.jimdo.com/miscellanea
/the-haunting-of-rf398/.

Tingley, Brett. "More World War II 'Ghost Planes' Sighted
Over Derbyshire, England." Mysterious Universe.
February 17, 2017. http://mysteriousuniverse
.org/2017/02/more-wwii-ghost-planes-sighted
-over-derbyshire-england/.

Notes:

- The section on phantom planes just scratches the
surface of the haunted history of World War II
phantom planes, especially in the UK. A good
collection of stories and accounts can be found here:
http://www.paranormaldatabase.com/aviation
/pages/avdata.php.

Chapter 3

Bradshaw, Danny. *Ghosts on the Battleship North Carolina.* Wilmington: Bradshaw Publishing Company, 2002.

Byers, Thomas. "The USS Arizona And Paranormal Activity." Hub Pages. Updated October 25, 2010. http://hubpages.com/religion-philosophy /The-USS-Arizona-And-Paranormal-Activity.

Curran, Erica Jackson. "Bruce Orr returns with tales of the unexplained aboard the USS Yorktown." *Charleston City Paper*, October 10, 2012. http://www.charlestoncitypaper.com /charleston/bruce-orr-returns-with-tales-of -the-unexplained-aboard-the-uss-yorktown /Content?oid=4201886.

Euston, Mickey. "A Maritime Haunting—The Ghosts of the USS Yorktown (CV-10)." *Scares and Haunts of Charleston* (blog). Accessed October 23, 2017. https://scaresandhauntsofcharleston.wordpress .com/2012/05/13/a-maritime-haunting-the -ghosts-of-the-uss-yorktown-cv-10/.

"Haunted Ships: The USS Lexington in Corpus Christi, Texas." Haunted Places to Go. Accessed October 24, 2017. http://www.haunted-places-to-go.com/haunted -ships-1.html.

Mills, Eric. *The Spectral Tide: True Ghost Stories of the U.S. Navy.* Annapolis: Naval Institute Press, 2009.

Morphy, Rob. "The Ghost Face of the USS
    Arizona." Mysterious Universe. October 6,
    2011. http://mysteriousuniverse.org/2011/10
    /the-ghost-face-of-the-uss-arizona/.

Orr, Bruce. *Ghosts of the USS Yorktown: The Phantoms of
    Patriots Point.* Charleston: The History Press, 2012.

"Pearl Harbor: The Ghost of the USS Arizona." Seeks
    Ghosts. December 7, 2012. https://seeksghosts.blogspot
    .com/2012/12/pearl-harbor-ghost-of-uss
    -arizona.html.

Perkins, Allison. "Haunted? USS North Carolina's Night
    Watchman Believes He Has Supernatural Shipmates."
    Greensboro News & Record. October 30, 2002.
    http://www.greensboro.com/haunted-uss-north
    -carolina-s-night-watchman-believes-he-has
    /article_1116386c-01c9-5409-8089-7ba5555c6b78.html.

Satterfield, John R. *We Band of Brothers: The Sullivans and
    World War II.* Parkersburg: Mid-Prairie Books, 1995.

Sham, Jon. "Ship of Lost Souls: Unexplained phenomena
    lead some workers at the Buffalo Naval Yard to
    believe in ghosts." Generation. Accessed July 7, 2017.
    Archived: http://web.archive.org/web/20071125125529
    /http://www.subboard.com/generation
    /articles/119308602991148.asp.

"The Polite Haunting of the USS Lexington." Winter Texans Online. Accessed October 24, 2017. http://wintertexansonline.com/polite-ghost -of-the-lady-lex.html.

"USS Hornet CV/CVA/CVS-12 Ghost Stories." ITS Caltech. https://www.its.caltech.edu/~drmiles /ghost_stories.html.

"USS The Sullivans." Haunted Houses. Accessed October 22, 2017. http://www.hauntedhouses.com/states /ny/uss-sullivans.htm.

Notes:

- Accounts also based on email interviews with members of Port City Paranormal and the group's thorough diary about their investigations on their website here: http://portcityparanormal.com /battleshipdiaries.html.

- Bedford Paranormal also reports on their investigations of possible paranormal activity on the Battleship *North Carolina* here: http://www.bedfordparanormal.com/Battleship _NorthCarolina.php.

- Many of the haunted ships in this book have their own ghost tours. Check out Yorktown Ghost Tours: http://www.yorktownghosttours.com/.

- This is an impressive spot for videos of some insights from one of the country's leading paranormal researchers and especially his investigations on the USS *Hornet*, a place he considers one of the most haunted spots on earth—or rather, at sea. The Early Show. 2001 Hornet clip. https://www.youtube.com /watch?v=VNTyFbP2AO8.

- Loyd Auerbach's YouTube site: https://www.youtube .com/channel/UCLRcFieyZjdJGD3U7e9Piwg.

Chapter 4

Freiss, Timothy. *Haunted Green Bay*. Charleston: The History Press, 2010. http://channel .nationalgeographic.com/killing-lincoln/articles /the-story-of-lincolns-ghost/.

Keane, David, and Nicola Oakley. "'Ghost of Sir Winston Churchill' photographed 'stalking' man on the London Underground." *The Mirror*, March 17, 2017. https://www.mirror.co.uk/news/weird-news /ghost-sir-winston-churchill-photographed-7575424.

Kiger, Patrick J. "The Story of Lincoln's Ghost." *National Geographic*, January 24, 2013.

"Legends and Ghost Stories of the Highland Inn (a grain of salt required …)." The Highland Inn. Last updated 2015. http://highland-inn.com/legends.html.

"MPIN Investigations." *Midwestern Paranormal Investigative Network* (blog). https://mpinetwork .wordpress.com/mpininvestigations/.

Nesbitt, Mark and Patty A. Wilson. *The Big Book of Pennsylvania Ghost Stories*. Mechanicsburg: Stackpole Books, 2008.

Nesbitt, Mark. *Civil War Ghost Trails: Stories from America's Most Haunted Battlefields*. Mechanicsburg: Stackpole Books, 2012.

Patton Totten, Ruth Ellen. *The Button Box: A Daughter's Loving Memoir of Mrs. George S. Patton*. Columbia: University of Missouri Press, 2005.

Powell IV, Lewis. "A Spectral Tour of the Shenandoah Valley." Southern Spirit Guide. September 29, 2014. http://www.southernspiritguide .org/a-spectral-tour-of-the-shenandoah-valley/.

Wittman, Scott. "Ghosts of The National Railroad Museum." *Mysterious Heartland* (blog). December 10, 2014. https://mysteriousheartland.com/2014/12/10 /ghosts-of-the-national-railroad-museum/.

Chapter 5

Fortune, Dion. *The Magical Battle of Britain*. Cheltenham, UK: Skylight Press, 2012.

Handwerk, Brian. "Will We Ever Know Why Nazi Leader Rudolf Hess Flew to Scotland in the Middle of World War II?" *Smithsonian*, May 10, 2016. http://www.smithsonianmag.com/history /will-we-ever-know-why-nazi-leader-rudolf -hess-flew-scotland-middle-world-war-ii -180959040/#W6y5ChDqT5cXLTa0.99.

Horowitz, Mitch. *Occult America: White House Seances, Ouija Circles, Masons, and the Secret Mystic History of Our Nation*. New York: Bantam, 2009.

Horowitz, Mitch. *One Simple Idea: How the Lessons of Positive Thinking Can Transform Your Life*. New York: Crown Publishing Group, 2014.

Kaczynski, Richard. *Perdurabo, Revised and Expanded Edition: The Life of Aleister Crowley*. Berkeley: North Atlantic Books, 2010.

Sable Aradia. "The Magical Battle of Britain." *Between the Shadows* (blog). Patheos. August 1, 2015. http:// www.patheos.com/blogs/betweentheshadows/2015/08 /the-magical-battle-of-britain/.

"Top 10 Crowley Myths which are Actually True." Aleister Crowley 2012. August 5, 2012. https://ac2012 .com/2012/08/05/aleister-crowley-myths-actually-true/.

Welton, Benjamin. "Occult Connections: The Strange Case of Ian Fleming, World War II, and Aleister Crowley." *Artistic Licence Renewed* (blog). July 23, 2014.

http://literary007.com/2014/07/23/occult-connections
-the-strange-case-of-ian-fleming-world-war-ii-and
-aleister-crowley/.

Chapter 6

Chamberlin, Jo. "The Foo Fighter Mystery,"
The American Legion, December, 1945.
Available here: http://www.project1947.com
/fig/1945a.htm#chamberlin.

Emery, David. "'Deadly Double' Pearl Harbor Mystery
Wasn't So Mysterious After All." Snopes. Accessed
December 7, 2017. http://www.snopes.com/2016/12
/07/deadly-double-pearl-harbor-mystery/.

"Foo Fighters of World War II." The Museum of
Unnatural Mystery. Accessed October 26, 2017.
http://www.unmuseum.org/foo.htm.

Gilbert, Val. "D-Day crosswords are still a few clues short
of a solution." *The Telegraph*, May 3, 2004.
http://www.telegraph.co.uk/news/uknews/1460892
/D-Day-crosswords-are-still-a-few-clues-short
-of-a-solution.html.

Johnson, Ben. "Crossword Panic of 1944." Historic UK.
History, Accessed October 26, 2017.
http://www.historic-uk.com/HistoryUK
/HistoryofBritain/Crossword-Panic-of-1944/.

"Legend of the Curse of Tamerlane: History, Facts and Myths." Advantour. Accessed October 26, 2017. http://www.advantour.com/uzbekistan/legends /tamerlane-curse.htm.

Littleton, C. Scott. "Eyewitness Account of The Battle of Los Angeles (PT. 1)." The UFO Chronicles. March 1, 2014. http://www.theufochronicles.com/2014/02 /eyewitness-account-of-battle-of-los.html.

Maloney, Mack. *UFOs in Wartime: What They Didn't Want You to Know*. New York: The Berkley Publishing Group, 2011.

Moore, William L., and Charles Berlitz. *The Philadelphia Experiment: Project Invisibility*. New York: Fawcett, 1995.

"The Great Los Angeles Air Raid of 1942." *Phantoms and Monsters* (blog). December 29, 2010. http://www.phantomsandmonsters.com/2010 /12/great-los-angeles-air-raid-of-1942.html.

"The Philadelphia Experiment From A-Z." *DE 173* (blog). Accessed October 26, 2017. http://www.de173.com/.

"War on words—the crossword panic of May 1944." *The Telegraph*, Accessed October 27, 2017. http://puzzles .telegraph.co.uk/site/article_full_details?article_id=16.

Notes:

- For a skeptical side of this case, check out the Skeptoid podcast: The Real Philadelphia Experiment. December 24, 2006. https://skeptoid.com/episodes/4016.

GET MORE AT **LLEWELLYN.COM**

Visit us online to browse hundreds of our books and decks, plus sign up to receive our e-newsletters and exclusive online offers.

- Free tarot readings • Spell-a-Day • Moon phases
- Recipes, spells, and tips • Blogs • Encyclopedia
- Author interviews, articles, and upcoming events

GET SOCIAL WITH **LLEWELLYN**

Find us on   🐦 @LlewellynBooks
www.Facebook.com/LlewellynBooks

GET BOOKS AT **LLEWELLYN**

LLEWELLYN ORDERING INFORMATION

Order online: Visit our website at www.llewellyn.com to select your books and place an order on our secure server.

Order by phone:
- Call toll free within the US at 1-877-NEW-WRLD (1-877-639-9753)
- We accept VISA, MasterCard, American Express, and Discover.
- Canadian customers must use credit cards.

Order by mail:
Send the full price of your order (MN residents add 6.875% sales tax) in US funds plus postage and handling to: Llewellyn Worldwide, 2143 Wooddale Drive, Woodbury, MN 55125-2989

POSTAGE AND HANDLING

STANDARD (US):
(Please allow 12 business days)
$30.00 and under, add $6.00.
$30.01 and over, FREE SHIPPING.

INTERNATIONAL ORDERS,
INCLUDING CANADA:
$16.00 for one book, plus $3.00 for each additional book.

Visit us online for more shipping options. Prices subject to change.

FREE CATALOG!

To order, call
1-877-
NEW-WRLD
ext. 8236
or visit our
website